The Sons of Zadok

THE SONS OF ZADOK

What Will You Do for 1000 Years?

Sermon in a Book Series
Volume 5

Evangelist Ken McDonald Th.M.

First Edition
©2022 Ken McDonald
All rights reserved

ISBN: 978-1-942769-17-0

All Rights Reserved. No part of this publication may be reproduced, stored in a retrieval system, or transmitted in any form by any means, electronic, mechanical, photocopy, recording, or otherwise, without the prior written permission of the publisher, except for brief quotations in critical reviews or articles.

All Scripture quotes are from the
King James Authorized Version of 1611

Cover designed by Ken and Terri Lee McDonald
Cover Photo: Shutterstock
www.everywordpublishing.com

Table of Contents

Preface	9
Introduction	11
Rightly Diving the Word of Truth	15
The Second Coming	39
Establishment of the Kingdom	79
The Sons of Zadok	93
The Christian	137
Obededom	181

Preface

I have tried to write this book in a way that all who read it will be able understand what I am writing about. It is possible that some who read this book will be new Christians or others who have never been discipled in the word of God. So I have tried to be thorough in my explanations.

For those of you who are well established in the faith, as well as in the word of God, there may be times the book is a bit *"tedious."* This is why.

Introduction

The following story was told to me by the Sunday school teacher of the class. He is now a Pastor.

It was Sunday morning and time for the church Sunday school class to begin. There was an even mix of boys and girls, this class was the teenage class. As often is the case, some of the teenagers wanted to be there, and some did not.

The teacher was a young man in his middle twenties who had been recently honorably discharged from the US Army. He had been a military police officer, and in spite of his strong military presence, he was kind and jokingly friendly to the kids. They liked him and responded to him well. He also had grown up in a home where his father was a pastor, so church was a very familiar place to him.

The class began as usual with prayer and then the study of the word of God. As discussion progressed it

The Sons of Zadok

evolved into talking about trials in the Christian life. Specifically, that if you live for the Lord, there are going to be trials that come your way.

For those in the class that really did not want to be there, the thought of trials coming their way if they would live for the Lord was only more reason to not live for Him in their mind. They wanted to have fun and enjoy their lives.

One of the girls in attendance that day was one who attended faithfully, but only her mother and she came to church. Her father and brothers, though claiming to be saved, did not come to church. The boys were following the poor example of their father. Coming from a spiritually split home, she was a bit confused and troubled in her thoughts. She longed to have her whole family in church together, as I am sure her mother longed and prayed for that as well. She raised her hand to ask the following question: *"If God is going to wipe away all tears from our eyes, then why are we trying so hard?"*

All of the kids looked at the teacher for his answer and he was briefly stumped. He knew her attitude was wrong as well as her reasoning, but he also was not satisfied with the answer he gave her. He told her that we should do right and serve the Lord out of a love for Jesus Christ. It is the right thing to do. And that is the right answer. But to a selfish, carnal Christian that answer is not enough to motivate them to do right. It was not the kind of answer that she could say to her father to motivate him to get back in church. It ought to, but there is no punishment in that answer. There is no warning as to what it will cost you for not doing

Introduction

right, for not living for and loving your Lord Jesus Christ.

Yes, if you truly are born again, then you are going to Heaven. You will not end up in Hell and then in the Lake of Fire.

> ^{37}Nay, in all these things we are more than conquerors through him that loved us.
>
> ^{38}For I am persuaded, that neither death, nor life, nor angels, nor principalities, nor powers, nor things present, nor things to come,
>
> ^{39}Nor height, nor depth, nor any other creature, shall be able to separate us from the love of God, which is in Christ Jesus our Lord. (Rom. 8:37-39)

Someone who has not been born again, and therefore is lost, is not in the love of God. Notice the word "*in.*" The Lord loved them on the cross but right now they are under the wrath of God.

> ^{36}He that believeth on the Son hath everlasting life: and he that believeth not the Son shall not see life; but **the wrath of God abideth on him.** (John 3:36)

If you are born again, one day all of your tears will be wiped away. Thank God! Amen!! But there is much for a Christian to lose. You not only will lose rewards at the Judgment Seat of Christ, but you will lose the joy and privilege of reigning with Jesus Christ for 1000 years.

For many Christians in this Laodicean, selfish time in which we live, they have the attitude just like that young girl's father in the Sunday school class. It is the

The Sons of Zadok

attitude of, *"I'm saved and going to Heaven. Great! That is settled, so now I can get on with my life. I will get the best of now and in eternity. Wow! This is great!"*

Remember this, the tears are not wiped away until the end of the Millennium, after the great White Throne Judgement. That's over 1000 years. That is something to think about!

Chapter 1

Rightly Diving the Word of Truth

¹⁵Study to shew thyself approved unto God, a workman that needeth not to be ashamed, **rightly dividing** the word of truth. (2 Tim. 2:15)

Have you ever had someone try to describe something to you, yet you couldn't picture in your mind what they were talking about? Whether their description was lacking, or it was just something that could not be described adequately, you were not able to picture, nor understand what they were talking about.

In the book of Nehemiah, and under the leadership of Nehemiah, a remnant of Israel had returned to the land of Israel. They had been in captivity for many years, but God had answered prayer and they were now back home. The city was in ruins, and the people worked hard to restore some semblance of organization to Jerusalem. Not only was it hard work, but they were risking their lives doing it as the enemies around the area were fighting them as well. It was a very hard time.

The Sons of Zadok

On the seventh month, the people came to Ezra the priest and requested for him to read the law to them. They wanted to hear the word of God. Ezra complied and a special platform was immediately built that elevated him so he could speak for all the people to hear. He stood up on it and read the law to the people who could understand it. Little children and such were not there. The distractions were kept to a minimum.

> [8] So they read in the book in the law of God distinctly, and gave the sense, and **caused them to understand the reading.** (Neh. 8:8)

Ezra and his helpers caused the people to understand the law. As the people listened to the law, they began to weep. But Nehemiah and Ezra spoke up and said to the people:

> [10] Then he said unto them, Go your way, eat the fat, and drink the sweet, and send portions unto them for whom nothing is prepared: for this day is holy unto our Lord: neither be ye sorry; **for the joy of the LORD is your strength.** (Neh. 8:10)

> [12] And all the people went their way to eat, and to drink, and to send portions, and to make great mirth, **because they had understood the words that were declared unto them.** (Neh. 8:12)

To understand the words of God is a great and wonderful thing. It is something that is impossible for a lost man to do.

> [14] But the natural man receiveth not the things of the Spirit of God: for they are foolishness unto him: neither can he know

them, **because they are spiritually discerned.** (1Cor. 2:14)

The Bible is a spiritual book. In order to understand the word of God, and therefore the things of God, you must have the Holy Spirit. In order to have the Holy Spirit, you must be born again. After the new birth, then you can begin to understand the Bible and all that God has for you.

Once upon a time there was a very simple man working alongside a friend of his. His friend suddenly dropped over dead. This simpleton kept trying to sit the man up as well as make him stand. When some others came around, they saw him trying his best to keep the dead man upright and heard him saying, *"He needs something inside him."*

It is that way with understanding the Bible. You need the Holy Spirit inside you. He gives man the understanding.

Along with the Holy Spirit, the Bible gives many types and metaphors in order to enable us to understand what the Lord is talking about. For example, one of the greatest metaphors in the Bible is of a Lamb. Our Lord is said to be the Lamb of God.

In the book of Exodus, the Passover lamb is a picture of the death of our Lord Jesus Christ. The Passover Lamb was killed. It's blood that was then "struck" upon the outside lintel of the doors of the houses of the Israelites, as well as any of the Egyptians who would listen to Moses. The visible blood of the Lamb caused the Lord to pass over the house so that the first born was not killed. It is a picture of a sinner being covered by the blood of the Lord Jesus Christ. That sinner, when

The Sons of Zadok

he dies will not go to Hell, but go straight to Heaven. The metaphor illustrates the truth so that you can better comprehend what is being taught. It is like windows that allow beams of light to shine in and illuminate the room so you can better see what is there.

In this chapter I am going to explain to you what the Millennium is, and when it will take place. I will try to use types and metaphors, as well as plain scriptures that tell what it is and when it will take place. Unfortunately in this day and age, the millennial time has not been clearly understood. Often the reason for this is the fact that the teachers of scripture have not rightly divided the word of God. The result is a faulty understanding of the scriptures which results in faulty doctrine.

When the Millennium is misunderstood, the result has been war, and I mean literal world war. Often the reason given for going to war is to bring in a great new world of peace and safety. The leaders will claim that they are going to bring in the kingdom of peace, but unfortunately all that happens is more wars come and go.

There is a simple truth that you must understand in regards to ending all wars on this earth, which is this:

[14]Glory to God in the highest, and on earth peace, good will toward men. (Luke 2:14)

There will *never* be peace on earth until there is glory to God in the highest *FIRST!*

Man wants to bring in the kingdom of peace without giving the glory to God in the highest first, and it will *NEVER* work. Righteousness always precedes peace.

In your heart there was no peace until righteousness

Rightly Dividing the Word of Truth

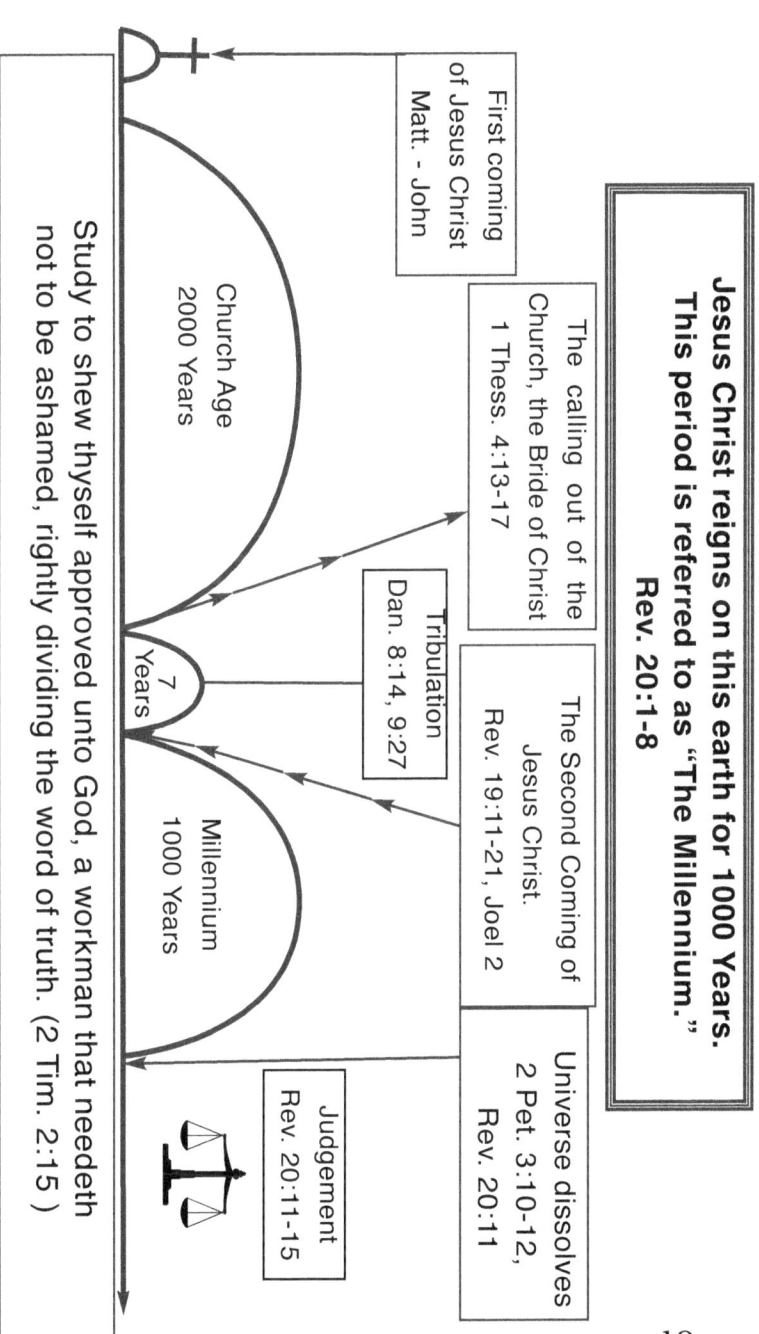

The Sons of Zadok

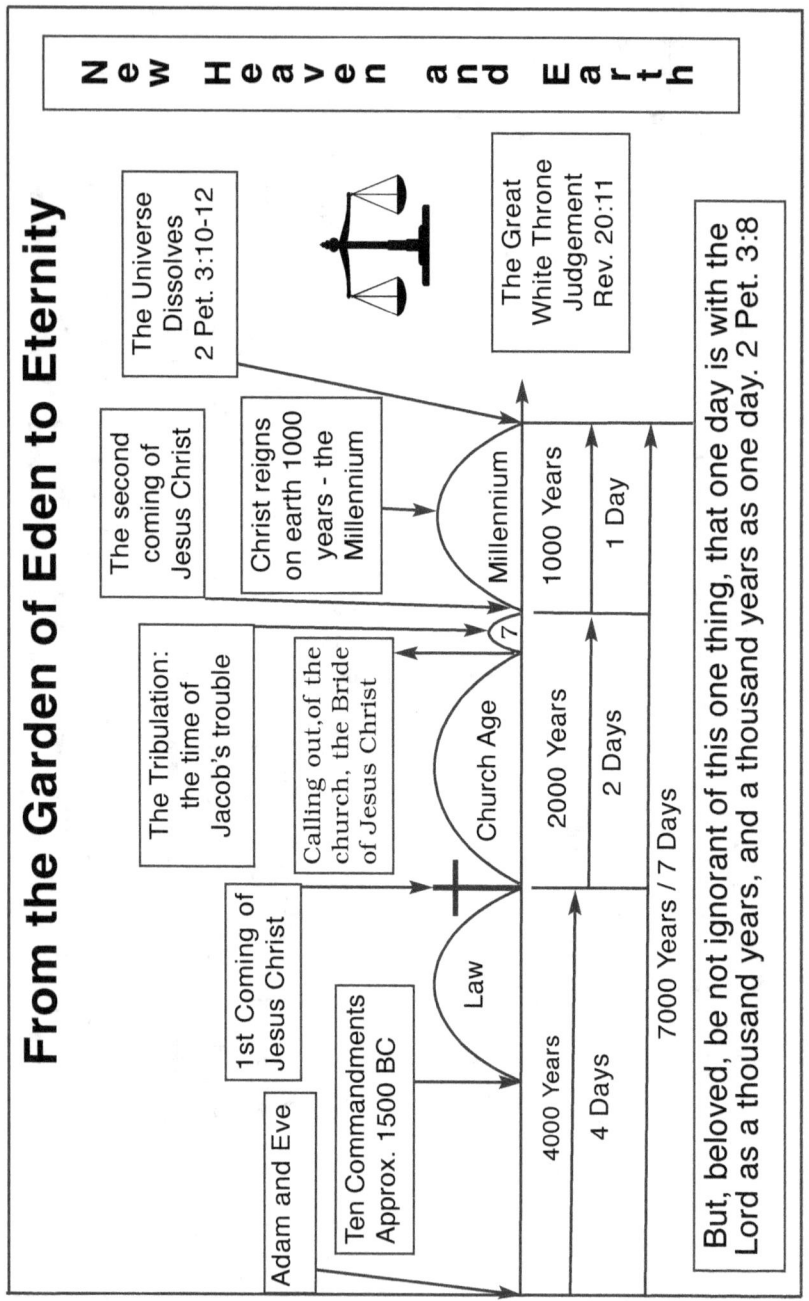

entered. Righteousness did not enter until the King of Righteousness entered you when you were born again. After that, you had- -and have- -peace. But if you allow sin to reign in your body, then you will lose your peace. The more sin you allow in your body, the less peace you have until you are completely miserable. If you repent and confess your sins to your Lord Jesus Christ, then the peace returns. There is no peace without righteousness first. That is an absolute truth. There is no way around it.

The main topic of this book is the Millennium. It is a kingdom of peace on earth for 1000 years. The reason for the peace is because the King of Peace, our Lord Jesus Christ, is ruling and reigning on this earth. Righteousness has come and thus peace ensues. It will be the greatest time ever on this earth, and with the help of God, I will try to explain when this is going to take place.

As you can see from the charts, this millennial kingdom takes place the last 1000 years of the existence of this earth. It is also the last 1000 years of this universe. As it has been said, "The best is yet to come!" The Millennium will be the crescendo of all time.

There is no doubt that the world we live in now has immense beauty. To view the stars on a clear night, and to see one shoot across the dark night sky and leave a sparkling trail behind it, is a beautiful sight. When the trail is bright and long, it is so spectacular that you might remember it for the rest of your life.

I grew up in Tuolumne County, California, which is nestled in the heart of the Sierra Nevada Mountains. A large section of the county is located inside the

The Sons of Zadok

boundaries of Yosemite National Park. Because of this proximity, I visited the park many times. One of the prettiest times, and most memorable sights for me in Yosemite was spring.

The most famous place in Yosemite is Yosemite Valley with its iconic sight of the Half Dome. Many professional wildlife and nature photographers claim the Yosemite Valley to be the most picturesque valley on earth. Along the sides of the valley are gray granite cliffs that shoot straight up almost 3000 feet. The valley is carpeted by lush green grass with the Merced river placidly flowing through the middle of it. The water is so clear that you can easily see the bottom, with its rounded stones and rainbow trout darting up and down under the water. Tall green pine, cedar, and fir trees grow and scent the air. As the breeze gently blows through their branches, a symphony of peace rings out. Chiming along with the concert are the joyful chirps of birds singing praises to God. Even the strange squawks of blue jays are fitting in the grand outdoor concert.

As you gaze upward to the tops of the cliffs, there are waterfalls pouring over the sides of the cliffs. Yosemite Falls, Bridal Veil Falls, Horsetail Falls to name a few. Their white, foamy waters plunge through the air and crash on the rocks below, which in turn sends a misty vapor of water into the air. As the sun shines on this mist, the light diffuses into rainbows of beauty. Beautiful wildflowers bloom from the crags on the side of the cliffs as well as amongst the green lush carpet of the valley floor. Yes, it is beautiful to say the least. And there are many, many other sights on this earth that

Rightly Dividing the Word of Truth

are as beautiful as well.

But realize this: what you are seeing now is under a curse. The curse that God placed on creation in Genesis 3. In the Millennium, that curse is going to be lifted. The animals will be vegetarian. (I guess that means no more mosquitoes and ticks. Glory!) The sun will shine seven times brighter, and thus the moon will be seven times brighter. The Bible says the light of the moon will be as the light of the day is now.

> [26] Moreover the **light of the moon shall be as the light of the sun**, and the light of the sun shall be sevenfold, as the light of seven days, in the day that the LORD bindeth up the breach of his people... (Is. 30:26)

Soooo, when will this be? Well... guess what? We are at the threshold of this event happening. Exactly when, I cannot say. But there are many clearly visible signs the Bible declares to take place right before the Lord Jesus Christ returns to this earth. (Keep in mind that the Christians are leaving seven years prior to our Lord's return.)

A few of the signs appearing right before our eyes are Israel becoming a nation in 1948, and the Jews have been returning to their homeland in droves. As in the days of Noah and Lot, there is now a prevalence of sodomy. The Bible speaks of a rise in earthquakes. Check it out, and you will see that earthquakes, and the intensity of them, have multiplied in the last 50 years. The Bible speaks of pestilence as a sign. Ever hear of COVID, Ebola, bird flue, or unexplained death of children with hepatitis? Wars and rumors of wars is

The Sons of Zadok

another sign, as well as a great falling away of Christianity.

It is not even a debate that Christianity today is spiritually polluted, and many churches are empty or without a pastor. As an evangelist, I have preached in many churches that have zero children in them; only people over 40 years old. There is a great falling away taking place, and it is a sign that this present church age is over, done, finished, kaput!! There will be no revival coming. It is not going to happen.

To write like this troubles some people who claim that a revival is getting ready to break out worldwide. No, it is not!!! Why? Because the overwhelming majority of churches are using corrupt Satanic bibles, using corrupt fleshly music, and the majority people of the churches are living corrupt, fleshly, sinful lives. What's more is that the vast majority of saints today have no idea what proper doctrine is. If you will study doctrine in the word of God, it has to do with, not just belief, but manner of life. Sound doctrine in the word of God is to live godly and clean. The signs are all around that we are at the end of the church age. Get ready, for Jesus Christ is coming any day now!

When the signs are compared with the biblical timeline, then you understand how close it really is. The timeline is very important if you want to understand the Millennium.

From the first couple Adam and Eve, unto the cross of Jesus Christ, is four thousand years. Some people will claim that the calendars have been changed and we don't know for sure what the date is. Well, if all you go by are the calendars, then yes, that would be a true statement. But there is something much more accurate than the calendars, that being the holy words of God. No, God does not tell us the *exact* time line, but God did that on purpose. Why? Because He tells us:

⁴⁴Therefore be ye also ready: for in such an hour as ye think not the Son of man cometh. (Matt. 24:44)

If man knew exactly when the Lord Jesus Christ would return, do you know what he would do? He would live wickedly right up until a few minutes before the Lord was to come, and then he would "get right with God." In other words, he would merely use God, like many do these days, to keep themselves out of Hell, but live like any other atheist around. But the word of God says that, "...**The just shall live by faith.**" (Rom. 1:17)

So no one knows exactly when the Lord will come. But there are biblical signs recorded in the word of God so that when you see these signs, then you know it will be soon.

A good illustration is that of a pregnant woman. You don't know exactly when the baby is coming, but you have signs that tell how close it is going to be. "Momma's belly" is getting bigger and bigger. Then preliminary contractions begin. But when the water breaks, you know it won't be long. The contractions get stronger and "momma" is in Labor. The baby is on the way. And to ignore the signs is foolish.

I did hear of a woman by the name of Lavinia Mounga, who was on a flight from Utah to Hawaii. She did not know that she was pregnant, but on the flight she went into Labor and gave birth to a son. Fortunately there

The Sons of Zadok

were three intensive care neo-natal nurses on board, as well as a general practice physician.

(Mom Who Didn't Know She Was Pregnant Gives Birth on a Plane to 29-Week-Old Baby, Lifenews.com May, 18, 2021)

How many people are living today not knowing that things could change in a moment! In less than a minute the entire world could change, and one day it will.

So from Genesis chapter one unto the birth of Jesus Christ is approximately 4000 years. In the Bible, this is likened unto four days.

> [8] But, beloved, be not ignorant of this one thing, that **one day *is* with the Lord as a thousand years, and a thousand years as one day.** (2 Pet. 3:8)

This would be Sunday, Monday, Tuesday, and Wednesday. The first four days of the week.

Then you have the Church Age. This starts at the cross, the death of the Testator, and proceeds for approximately 2000 years. (For those of you who would argue about the specific time the church started...relax. I am explaining this in general terms for simplicity.) This 2000 years would be—and spiritually are—Thursday and Friday.

Then there is a little blip called the Tribulation, or some would call it the Great Tribulation. (Yeah, yeah, whatever!) It is the time of Jacob's Trouble and also called Daniel's 70th week. It is seven years long and takes place right after the end of the Church Age, and right before the Millennium.

The Millennium is 1000 years long or one day. It

would correspond to the seventh day of rest which would be Saturday. The whole timeline is one week, with the days Sunday through Saturday each being 1000 years long.

> [4]For a thousand years in thy sight are *but as* yesterday when it is past, and *as* a watch in the night. (Psa. 90:4)

The number seven in the word of God is the number of completion. When God does something, He often will do it by sevens. When the seventh is reached, whatever God is doing is done. When the eighth comes, it is a new beginning. The seventh day of the week ends the week. The eighth day is the beginning of a new week.

In this time that we live in, there is an attempt to change all things that have been set up by the Creator. Boys are trying to be girls and girls are trying to be boys, good is bad and bad is good, and so on. It is a time of manifest rebellion against all that is established by God. The result of this is confusion, and God is not the author of it.

When the Anti-Christ shows up, he is going to change times and laws.

> [25]And he shall speak *great* words against the most High, and shall wear out the saints of the most High, and **think to change times and laws**... (Dan. 7:25)

He will try to eliminate this seven system and thus create much confusion. This will take place during that seven years of tribulation.

So God does things by seven, meaning seven is the number of completion. In Genesis 1 there are the seven

The Sons of Zadok

days of creation. Those days are not one thousand years each. How do you know that? Because it says the evening and the morning were the first day, the second day and so on. Those days are 24 hour periods. But the seventh day God rested from his Labor.

> ⁵And God called the light Day, and the darkness he called Night. And the **evening and the morning** were the first day. (Gen. 1:5)

In the book of Revelation there are seven churches mentioned with Laodicea being the last one. (Rev. 2-3) (That is the church period we are in now.) There are also the seven trumpets (Rev. 8:2), the seven vials (Rev. 15:7), and seven last plagues (Rev. 15:6). There are the seven Spirits of God (Rev. 3:1, Isa. 11:2). Also the candlestick that sits in the tabernacle of God has seven golden pipes through which the oil flows (Zech. 4:2).

The Bible claims that God created man on the sixth day out of the dust of the earth (Sixth day Gen. 1:23-1:31).

> ⁷And the LORD God formed man *of* the dust of the ground, and breathed into his nostrils the breath of life; and man became a living soul. (Gen. 2:7)

So your body has two legs, two arms, a head and the torso. That makes six parts; then God breathed into man's nostrils the breath of life, and man became a living soul. When you add the soul you have a complete person, and thus he has seven parts to him.

But if a person gets born again, then they have a new birth, and a new life which is the eighth part of them. It is a new beginning.

In music there are seven major notes. The eighth note is an octave above the first and is a new beginning of the next octave.

Enoch is said to be the seventh from Adam, and God took him. Right after God took Enoch, there was a worldwide flood. Noah is said to be the eighth.

> ⁵And spared not the old world, but saved **Noah the eighth *person***, a preacher of righteousness, bringing in the flood upon the world of the ungodly; (2 Pet. 2:5)

These are just a few of the examples of God doing things by seven. There are more, but it illustrates the truth that God does things by sevens. And the last seven, at least in regard to seven days, is the seventh day of rest. That seventh day of rest, as far as the earth is concerned, is the 1000 years long Millennium.

THE CHURCH AGE

If you have looked at the charts, then you can see that according to the charts we are at the end of the church age. But how do we know that? How do we know that there are not another 50,000 years to go before the Lord comes?

The 4,000 years before the cross are established. There is no room to ignore this fact. As I said before, and I don't mean to repeat myself, but there may be some discrepancy in the 4,000 years, but only a few hundred at most, if you go by the word of God, a King James 1611 Bible.

There were wise men that came to see Jesus Christ

The Sons of Zadok

after His birth. They were able to figure out when and where He would be born within two to three years accuracy. I remember doing this very thing in Bible school and figuring out when the Lord would be born, using only the Old Testament scriptures. It can be done. If things and calendars were off by large amounts of time, then it would not come out right. But with the word of God, and going by the calendar, it does work out within two years, when Jesus Christ was born, and where He would be born.

> [16] Then Herod, when he saw that he was mocked of the wise men, was exceeding wroth, and sent forth, and slew all the children that were in Bethlehem, and in all the coasts thereof, **from two years old and under, according to the time which he had diligently enquired of the wise men.** (Matt. 2:16)

If you bring in books that are written by man, then there will be all kinds of confusion. But according to the word of God, 4000 years took place from the creation of man unto the first coming of Jesus Christ. You know what is interesting about that?

In Genesis one, on the fourth day came the sun, which is a clear type of Jesus Christ, the Light of the world. Then on the fifth day came life. You see, between the fourth and the fifth day, there is the cross upon which Jesus died. After the cross, the end of the fourth day, life appears on the fifth day. Life that will last forever. This is the beginning of the church. Does that mean no one was alive spiritually in the Old

Rightly Dividing the Word of Truth

Testament? No! But they had to wait in Paradise, which up until the resurrection of Jesus Christ, was in the heart of the earth.

I know Hell is in the heart of the earth, but Paradise was placed in a close proximity to Hell, since the rich man could yell over to Abraham and talk to him about Lazarus (Luke 16). There was a great gulf between the two places. But when the blood of Christ was shed on the Cross, it opened the way. Paradise, with all of its inhabitants, was translated up to Heaven. How do I know that? Because Paul was caught up into Paradise in 2 Corinthians 12. It's no longer in the heart of the earth.

> ³And I knew such a man, (whether in the body, or out of the body, I cannot tell: God knoweth;)
>
> ⁴How that **he was caught up into paradise**, and heard unspeakable words, which it is not lawful for a man to utter. (2Cor. 12:3-4)

So yes, the Old Testament saints had eternal life. But that life was fully possessed only after the Cross.

There are 4000 years, which is four days, before the Cross. The Cross marks the first coming of Jesus Christ. We also know that the last 1000 years is the Millennium. That only leaves 2000 years. Thus the church age can only be 2000 years, or 2 days long. There is no other way to get around it. With this understood (see previous charts), notice some interesting "coinky-dinks" in the word of God.

When God divides the number seven in the word of God, He will divide it into either by six parts and one

The Sons of Zadok

part, or He will divide it into four parts and three parts. Rarely does he ever divide it into five parts and two parts. So the types I have given have been the six days and one day when referring to the days of the week. The first day to the sixth day is grouped together, and then the Sabbath is all by itself. That makes six and one.

The following types will be the four parts and three parts. The cross started the two days of the church age, and then there is the one day of the Millennium. You will see this in the following Bible stories where the term "*two days*" is used. It will picture the Church age, and the two thousand years that the nation of Israel is out of fellowship with God.

In the fourth chapter of the gospel of John there is a story about Jesus saying that "he must needs go through Samaria." While in Samaria, He sits down by a well and ends up talking to a Samaritan woman. These are half-breed people made up of Jew and Gentile. (It is interesting to note that the church, the body of Christ, consists of Jews and Gentiles.) So He talks to her and *she believes Him.* This Gentile Samaritan woman then goes into the city and says,

> [29]Come, see a man, which told me all things that ever I did: is not this the Christ? (John 4:29)
>
> [40]So when the Samaritans were come unto him, they besought him that he would tarry with them: and **he abode there two days.** (John 4:40)

Jesus abode there *"two days,"* making it plainly a type of the church age.

Rightly Dividing the Word of Truth

In John chapter 11 is found the story of Lazarus who is a type of the nation of Israel. In this story Lazarus is sick and ends up dead. The nation Israel, at the time of the earthly life of Jesus Christ, was spiritually sick and at the point of death. Not long after the resurrection of Jesus Christ, the nation of Israel goes spiritually dead and stays dead for almost 2000 years.

> [7]For there is hope of a tree, if it be cut down, **that it will sprout again**, and that the tender branch thereof will not cease.
>
> [8]Though the root thereof wax old in the earth, and the stock thereof die in the ground;
>
> [9]Yet through the scent of water it will bud, and bring forth boughs like a plant.
> (Job 14:7-9)

World War 1 got the land of Palestine ready for the Jews with the Balfour Declaration, November 2, 1917. Then came World War 2 which ended in 1945, and it got the Jews ready to return to the land of Palestine. In 1948 Israel became a nation again, and the fig tree started to sprout once more. This is a very big sign that we are in the last days.

Lazarus becomes very sick, and his sisters send for Jesus to come and heal him. But when Jesus receives the news, He doesn't leave immediately. Even though the Bible says that Jesus loved Lazarus and his two sisters, yet He delays on purpose for *two days.*

> [3]Therefore his sisters sent unto him, saying, Lord, behold, he whom thou lovest is sick.
> (John 11:3)

Maybe you have prayed for the Lord's help, and He

The Sons of Zadok

didn't come through for you in time. It may hurt greatly, and it may seem like God has forsaken you, but trust Him. He has much greater plans for you than you can fully imagine. As an old colored preacher once said, "Heaven am da place of undastandin', earth am da place fo' trust!"

> ⁶When he had heard therefore that he was sick, **he abode two days still** in the same place where he was.
>
> ⁷Then after that saith he to *his* disciples, **Let us go into Judaea again.** (John 11:6-7)

For two thousand years the Lord has gone to the Gentiles. If a Jew wants to go to Heaven, he has to enter the very same way a "Gentile dog" enters, which is through the blood of Jesus Christ by the new birth. And, yes, there has been a remnant of Jews that have trusted Jesus Christ as their own personal Saviour. But notice the wording in verse 7: after the two days, **"Let us go into Judaea again."** The Jews are brought back into fellowship with God during the seven-year Tribulation. Jesus Christ returns to Judaea at His Second Coming. The Jews are then with Him in Jerusalem for 1000 years, during the Millennium. There is a lot in those two little verses!

In the book of Esther, the word "God" or "Lord" is never found. It is the only book in the Bible like that. In the book of Esther, Israel is in captivity under Gentile rule. It is a picture of the Church Age. Israel is greatly persecuted and hated in the book of Esther. As the book starts out, the King is married to a Gentile woman by the name of Vashti. But Vashti is rebellious and won't obey the King. It is very similar to this day and time of the Church Age where the Church, as a whole, is in complete rebellion to the Lord Jesus Christ.

The Church has lost her power and influence in the world and is completely apostate. There was a time when the governments feared the pulpits, but now the pulpits fear the governments. The time of the Church is over. The Church, as a body, is a geriatric body wheezing her last gasp. She props herself up with artificial supports because she no longer has the strength to stand on her own.

The Gentile queen Vashti, which is a type of the Church, is rebellious against her king and throws a party of her own. She won't obey the King's call. The king removes her from being the queen and a Jewish queen is installed. It is a picture of the Tribulation time when Israel is returned into favor with her God. Then notice the following:

> [1]Now it came to pass on **the third day**, that Esther put on *her* royal *apparel*, and stood in the inner court of the king's house, over against the king's house: and the king sat upon his royal throne in the royal house, over against the gate of the house.
>
> [2]And it was so, when the king saw Esther the queen standing in the court, *that* **she obtained favour in his sight**: and the king held out to Esther the golden sceptre that was in his hand. So Esther drew near, and touched the top of the sceptre. (Esth. 5:1-2)

Thus a picture of Israel, the bride of God the Father,

coming back into fellowship with her King. The wicked Haman is a type of the Anti-Christ who is hung, just like Judas. After two days, Israel is revealed to the world who she truly is.

There is one more that is very plain to see. It is found in Hosea:

> ^{15}I will go *and* return to my place, till they acknowledge their offence, and seek my face: **in their affliction they will seek me early.** (Hos. 5:15)
>
> ^{1}Come, and let us return unto the LORD: for he hath torn, and he will heal us; he hath smitten, and he will bind us up.
>
> ^{2}**After two days will he revive us: in the third day he will raise us up, and we shall live in his sight.** (Hos. 6:1-2)

In Hosea here, this is prophetically talking about Israel, and shows how they have gotten away from God. "Their affliction" will take place during the seven year tribulation, after the Church Age. Notice verse two: **"After two days will he revive us."** That is a picture of after the two thousand years of the Church Age. The nation of Israel, spiritually, is dead. I am talking spiritually. Physically the nation will always be God's people, but during the church age they are not in fellowship with their God. That will change after the church age.

"**In the third day he will raise us up...**" That third day is the Millennium, and Israel will be in their land with David reigning over them as their king. Jesus Christ will be in the temple at Jerusalem ruling and reigning over the world. Then, because righteousness has finally arrived on earth, there will be one thousand years of peace on this earth.

Along with the Lord Jesus Christ reigning will be His "wife" with him. That is His church. If you are born again, then you are part of His church and you are going to be married to the King of the universe, the Most High God, The Lord Jesus Christ. WOW!!!

So, what are you going to do for one thousand years?

The Sons of Zadok

Chapter 2

The Second Coming

The Christians

I am writing this book in the year 2022. We are at the end of the Church Age. Christianity is falling apart and the people are spiritually falling away. Just how much further do we have until the trumpet sounds and we are called out of here? I have no idea. All I know is that the signs are getting more and stronger every day. But if the Lord Jesus Christ comes today, then what you are about to read will take place seven years from the Rapture.

Jesus came the first time as a baby in a manger, born of the Virgin Mary. He lived a perfect sinless life and died on the Cross to pay for the sins of the world.

> [29]The next day John seeth Jesus coming unto him, and saith, Behold the Lamb of God, which taketh away the sin of the world. (John 1:29)

The Sons of Zadok

This was His first coming. But He told us,

> ³And if I go and prepare a place for you, **I will come again**, and receive you unto myself; that where I am, *there* ye may be also. (John 14:3)

Our Lord promised to come again, and so He will. The first part of His coming is for His Bride, the Church. This is commonly referred to as the Rapture, or calling out of the Church. At the Rapture Jesus Christ does not set His feet upon the earth. Seven years later He descends from Heaven, steps on the earth and takes over. At this first phase of His second coming though, we rise and meet Him in the air.

> ¹⁶For the Lord himself shall descend from heaven with a shout, with the voice of the archangel, and with the trump of God: and **the dead in Christ shall rise first:**
>
> ¹⁷Then we which are alive *and* remain shall be **caught up together with them in the clouds, to meet the Lord in the air:** and so shall we ever be with the Lord. (1Thess. 4:16-17)

The Rapture is said to be our Blessed Hope, and the truth of the Lord coming and calling us out of this world is to be a comfort to us. It most certainly is a comfort to think that we may never die. If Jesus Christ comes as you read this book, and if you are born again, then you will never die. You will be instantly changed into your new body and ascend to meet the greatest Lover and Friend that you have ever known.

It is an event that is very pleasant to imagine and think about. What will it be like?

It will happen very fast, for we are changed in the

moment, in the twinkling of an eye. Both the dead in Christ and those of us who are alive will be changed at the same time. Then we shall ascend into the clouds to meet our Lord in the air. How quickly we ascend I am not sure. In Acts chapter 1 the Lord ascends and they watched Him as He arose up into the sky.

For a type of the Rapture there is the translation of Enoch. When Enoch was translated he was there one minute and gone the next. To the world it will be like that. We will literally be gone in a moment. Amen! Even so come Lord Jesus!

Then, we will appear at the judgement seat of Christ in Heaven. During this time, there will be seven years of tribulation that take place on this earth. It is the time of Jacob's rouble, not the Church's trouble. Jacob is Israel; on the earth during this time, Israel will be persecuted greatly, but also brought back into fellowship with God the Father.

Up in Heaven, it is a different event. It is the judgement seat of Christ. If you are born again, then you are going to stand before Jesus Christ and give an account of how you lived after you were saved. It is a judgement, not for whether you are going to Heaven or Hell, but a judgement for rewards. Rewards that are to be given for the things that you did for Jesus Christ after you were saved.

> [12] So then every one of us shall give account of himself to God. (Rom. 14:12)
>
> [10] For we must all appear before the judgment seat of Christ; that every one may receive the things *done* in *his* body, according to that he

The Sons of Zadok

hath done, whether *it be* good or bad.
(2 Cor. 5:10)

Jesus is not mad at you when you stand at that time, or probably kneel, before Him. But it will be obvious whether you loved and served Him or not. If you loved and lived for yourself now, instead of loving and living for your Saviour in this life, it will be made manifest. It is best to remember that this life is but a vapor and will vanish away in a moment. If you spend your life living for now, then you will miss what the Lord wants to give you, and you will be ashamed one day.

There is a story in the Bible that illustrates clearly when someone lives for the moment and not in the light of eternity. It is the story of Esau.

Esau's grandfather was Abraham. God gave Abraham a promise, and that promise was that God would bless everyone that blessed Abraham, and curse everyone that cursed him. Abraham was the father of Isaac, and Isaac was the father of Esau and Jacob. Esau, because he was the firstborn, was in line to receive the blessing. But spiritual things did not mean much to Esau.

One day Esau had been out hunting and when he came in from the field, he was at the point of fainting. Coming in, he smelled some pottage that Jacob was cooking and told Jacob to give him some. But Jacob was a man with a spiritual eye. He saw his chance and told Esau that he would give him some pottage only if Esau sold him the birthright. To Jacob the birthright was very valuable, but it didn't mean much to Esau, especially since Esau was hungry. So for a moment of comfort in his belly, Esau sacrificed a permanent blessing on the altar of an immediate pleasure. Esau

The Second Coming

sold Jacob his birthright for a bowl of pottage.

Esau's lack of respect for spiritual things, and thus the selling of his birthright, brought him the following testimony from God the Father,

> [13] As it is written, Jacob have I loved, but **Esau have I hated.** (Rom. 9:13)

Not only that, but when it came time to receive the blessing, Esau weeps because he does not get the blessing. It was Esau's fault, yet Esau blames Jacob and claims Jacob stole his blessing. No, Esau sold out in a time when he was uncomfortable.

While a Christian cannot lose their salvation, yet there is a temptation to sell out for temporal convenience and comfort. If you do right, you are going to have trials. Consider the following account.

In the year 1499, one Badram, a pious man, was brought before the bishop of Norwich, having been accused by some of the priests, with holding the doctrines of Wickliffe. He confessed he did believe everything that was objected against him. For this, he was condemned as an obstinate heretic, and a warrant was granted for his execution; accordingly he was brought to the stake at Norwich, where he suffered with great constancy.

(AN ACCOUNT OF THE PERSECUTIONS IN GREAT BRITAIN AND IRELAND, PRIOR TO THE REIGN OF QUEEN MARY I, Foxe's Book of Martyrs)

So the temptation for a Christian is to give in to the world. To not live, according to the world; too *"extreme."* Just get along and don't make waves. Be nice, sweet,

The Sons of Zadok

and gentle. And in this age the vast majority of Christians are living just like that. They have done what Esau did. They sacrificed the permanent on the altar of the immediate. They have sacrificed very great rewards "tomorrow" so they can have comfort today. But one day, they will weep.

In a way, that is what this book is all about. Will you live in the light of eternity, or in the context of this book, in the light of the Millennium? Or will you sell out to the world, the flesh, and the devil? You have a free will, and God has given you the liberty to choose on your own. Christian, never sacrifice the permanent on the altar of the immediate.

In this Laodicean age in which we live, Christians are selling out for material things, instead of putting Jesus Christ first. Instead of living "poor," they turn their back on Jesus Christ and live to make money, live for the acquisition of material things. Then after they acquire their things, they use those things as evidence they are right with, and have been blessed, by God.

> ^{15}I know thy works, that thou art neither cold nor hot: I would thou wert cold or hot.
> ^{16}So then because thou art lukewarm, and neither cold nor hot, I will spue thee out of my mouth.
> ^{17}Because thou sayest, I am rich, and increased with goods, and have need of nothing; and knowest not that thou art wretched, and miserable, and poor, and blind, and naked... (Rev. 3:15-17)

It makes God want to puke (vs 16). Are you a Christian that makes God sick? God will never hate you, for if you are born again, then you are in the love of God. But you can become a Christian that God quits dealing with, and when that happens, you are in a mess.

> [19] As many as I love, I rebuke and chasten: be zealous therefore, and repent. (Rev. 3:19)

Why does God get this way? Because his child has sold out for temporal pleasure. You have become your own god. Covetousness is idolatry, and you are now an idolater. His command is to be zealous and repent!

In the story of Esau (Gen. 27) you will notice that Isaac is not mad at Esau. Isaac wanted to help him but couldn't. Esau had messed up his own reward. It was no one's fault but his own. Esau was mad at Jacob, and he blamed Jacob, but when all was said and done, it was Esau who blew it.

Many will condemn Jacob for lying about being Esau. Yes, Jacob did wrong, even though he was following his mother's command. Yes, Jacob, and his mother Rebekah, should have trusted the Lord and waited for God to work it out. But do not forget that God says, **"Jacob have I loved, but Esau have I hated."** (Rom. 9:13)

Now Christian, ever since you were born again you have been constructing a building in Heaven.

> [11] For other foundation can no man lay than that is laid, which is Jesus Christ.
>
> [12] Now **if any man build upon this foundation** gold, silver, precious stones, wood, hay, stubble;
>
> [13] Every man's work shall be made manifest: for the day shall declare it, because it shall

be revealed by fire; and the fire shall try every man's work of what sort it is.
¹⁴If any man's work abide which he hath built thereupon, he shall receive a reward.
¹⁵If any man's work shall be burned, he shall suffer loss: but he himself shall be saved; yet so as by fire. (1 Cor. 3:11-15)

You are going to stand before Jesus Christ. There will be some sort of building there that was constructed from your works on earth when you were saved. Some of that building will be wood, hay and stubble. And hopefully, some of it will be gold, silver and precious stones. There is a fire that it passes through and whatever comes out on the other side of the fire, you will get a reward for.

¹⁴His head and *his* hairs *were* white like wool, as white as snow; and **his eyes *were* as a flame of fire;** (Rev. 1:14)

I have heard it said that the Lord Jesus Christ will look at your works with His fiery eyes and burn up the wood, hay and stubble. That may be true. But one way or another, fire is there and the wood, hay and stubble is going to be burned up. If you have anything left, then you will receive a reward for it.

A girl in her late teens put on a fake diamond necklace and headed out the door to a dance on a Friday evening. As she walked through the living room to the front door, her younger sister was sitting on the couch reading her Bible. She looked up and said, *"You can wear that fake necklace now, but I am going to get a real one at the judgement seat of Christ."*

As C.T. Studd said, *"Only one life, 'twill soon be past.*

The Second Coming

Only what's done for Christ will last." How true that is!

Treasures in Heaven are only laid up when treasures on earth are laid down.

How long will it take to be judged? I don't know!

But it will happen, and you are going to give account to your Lord Jesus Christ. He will hold out His nail scarred hands. It will be obvious He loved and died for you. And it will also be obvious if you loved and carried your cross for Him. There will be no need for a verbal rebuke. You will know that whatever you end up with, or without, will be just and right.

Whether or not the judgement is public or private, I do not know for sure. But when the judgement is over, it will be plain for all to see exactly what kind of Christian you were.

Can we all do better? Absolutely! Should we all do our best? Yes! Are you trying to do your best? Is there something that you know your Lord Jesus Christ wants you to do, but you are not doing it? Oh, it may cost you a house, or a job, or an inheritance, but Jesus Christ is worth far more than any of those temporary things!

There will be no gloating by those who have more. There will be no competition amongst the saints, for then we will have perfect hearts and bodies. All pride, self and sin will be gone. The only one who will regret it will be you. And you will have over 1000 years to live with it, but remember it will also be public for 1000 years.

Last week something happened that is occurring less and less. A man that I know had a very good job as a lineman. It is a dangerous job, but one that pays well, and he was set, as they say, for life. He had been a

The Sons of Zadok

lineman for eleven years, but God had dealt with his heart when he was eleven years old and called him to preach. He knew he was called to preach. Now, he is married with a lovely wife and three beautiful children.

At one point in his life, before he was married, he had gotten away from the Lord and ended up crashing his truck by running off a bridge at night. The wrecked truck, with every window smashed out, looked like no one could have survived. As airbag dust settled in the truck, he got his bearings and found himself looking up at the stars through a broken-out windshield. He prayed and said, *"Well, God, you got me looking up at you. You got my attention."* From then on he started living for the Lord.

This past week, he quit his job, and has gone full time into the ministry. In order to save some money, he went to a gym to see about closing out his membership. When the lady behind the counter asked why, he told her that he had quit his job and is pastoring a church.

She looked at him and walked around the counter and gave him a polite hug. She then said, *"Thank you! You don't hear of men doing that anymore."* No, you don't! But remember this, the worth of something is how much it cost. How much your Christianity has cost you will determine its worth.

The bride of Christ, the Church, is going to have all her wrinkles ironed out. Every spot and blemish is going to be dealt with. And once that is done, then comes a very exciting time for us all. Then begins our Lord's triumphant return to take over all this earth. Coming back with Him will be His bride, the Church, as well as the saints from the Old Testament.

The Second Coming

There are three main battles that take place at the second coming of our Lord Jesus Christ. There is the battle at Petra, the battle at Jerusalem, and the battle in the valley of Megiddo. There is no doubt about these three battles. What I do not have as an absolute is the order in which these three battles take place. I am going to place them as Petra first, Jerusalem second and Megiddo third.

I think this is the order, but I think it strange that the Lord would enter Jerusalem, take over and sit down on His throne, only to leave and go to Megiddo for the final battle. It just seems odd to me. But the battle at Megiddo, or the battle of Armageddon, does seem to be the last battle. Perhaps He fights it, then returns to Jerusalem, and then sits down on the throne of the kingdom.

So the order of these battles, to me, is unclear, but the fact of these battles is very clear. They will take place and if you are saved, you will be a part of these battles.

To start with, there will be these beautiful white horses in Heaven. They will have been prepared for the war, and are eagerly anticipating the return. They shimmer in the light of Heaven. They paw on the golden streets and snort with excitement.

> ^{14}And the armies *which were* in heaven followed him upon **white horses**, clothed in fine linen, white and clean. (Rev. 19:14)

What you are getting ready to read about is the major

The Sons of Zadok

theme of the Bible. There are far more references in the Bible on the second coming of Christ than there are on the first coming. Why? Because the day God's Son got murdered at the hands of wicked men is not the highlight of the Bible to God the Father.

For you and I, as sinners deserving of Hell, it can be viewed as our highlight. Jesus Christ dying on the cross, being buried, and rising from the dead after three days and nights paid the price for our sins. Because of it, we get to go to Heaven if we have trusted Jesus Christ as our personal Saviour. Yes, the cross is the great highlight for sinners. I am not sure, but it is something like three or four to one, for every reference to the first coming there are three or four references to the second coming of Jesus Christ.

Excitement builds throughout all of Heaven. Shouts and praise to the Lord our God ring out as the event of all the ages is getting ready to take place. We join in on the praising of our God. Babylon has now fallen and it won't be long before our God, the rightful King of the universe comes and takes over what is rightly His.

> ^{2}And he cried mightily with a strong voice, saying, **Babylon the great is fallen, is fallen,** and is become the habitation of devils, and the hold of every foul spirit, and a cage of every unclean and hateful bird. (Rev. 18:2)

As I got ready to write about us returning with our Lord to this earth, this thought occurred to me, *"How do I know we return with the Lord to this earth?"* I have heard that for decades, and I have read many scriptures that seems to point to the fact that we return with

The Second Coming

Jesus Christ to this earth, but I thought that I would "nail it down" right here, before I go any further.

In Revelation 19 it says that, "**¹⁴The armies which were in Heaven followed him on white horses.**" Am I in one of those armies? If you are saved, are you in one of those armies? Well, let's see. What do we know?

We know that we are going to be caught out of this world and forever be with our Lord (1 Thess. 4:14-17). We know that after the Rapture, there is going to be on the earth a time of great tribulation. (To be exact, 2300 days Dan. 8:14). During that time in Heaven, the Church (i.e., saved people), is going to be judged at the judgement seat of Christ. Then at the end of the Tribulation, Jesus Christ is going to return to this earth and set up His kingdom for 1000 years. These things we know and can be easily found, so now let's study and see if we are in one of those armies that returns with our Lord Jesus Christ.

First of all, we are told that after the Rapture, it is written "**...And so shall we ever be with our Lord.**"

> ¹⁷Then we which are alive *and* remain shall be caught up together with them in the clouds, to meet the Lord in the air: and **so shall we ever be with the Lord.** (1 Th. 4:17)

There is no doubt that the Church is the bride of Christ when you read Ephesians 5.

> ³⁰For **we are members of his body, of his flesh, and of his bones.**
>
> ³¹For this cause shall a man leave his father and mother, and shall be joined unto his wife, and they two shall be one flesh.
>
> ³²This is a great mystery: but **I speak**

51

concerning Christ and the church. (Eph. 5:30-32)

So it can be easily seen that the Church will be with Jesus Christ on this earth since that is where He will be. We are His bride, thus He wants His bride with Him. Amen!

The fact that we will be on this earth during the Millennium is evident as well. Reigning with Jesus Christ is one of the rewards that a Christian earns. (I will be going into great detail on this later in this book.)

To be on this earth during the Millennium is said to be part of the *"first resurrection."* If you are saved, then you are already seated in heavenly places in Christ Jesus (Eph. 2:6) and you will never die. Going up in the Rapture is part of the first resurrection.

> [6] Blessed and holy *is* he that hath part in the first resurrection: on such the second death hath no power, but they shall be priests of God and of Christ, and **shall reign with him a thousand years.** (Rev. 20:6)

Now, notice the following portion of scripture. It is a bit lengthy, but it is all one sentence. I wanted to include it so as to get the context.

> [5] *Which is* a manifest token of the righteous judgment of God, that ye may be counted worthy of the kingdom of God, for which ye also suffer:
>
> [6] Seeing *it is* a righteous thing with God to recompense tribulation to them that trouble you;
>
> [7] And to you who are troubled rest with us, when **the Lord Jesus shall be revealed from**

The Second Coming

heaven with his mighty angels,
8In flaming fire taking vengeance on them that know not God, and that obey not the gospel of our Lord Jesus Christ:
9Who shall be punished with everlasting destruction from the presence of the Lord, and from the glory of his power;
10When he shall come to be glorified in his saints, and to be admired in all them that believe (because our testimony among you was believed) in that day. (2 Thess. 1:5-10)

When you read, ..."**flaming fire**..." in verse 8, it is a reference to the Second Advent. It is not a reference to the Rapture because at the Rapture there is no flaming fire, there are clouds. Not only that, but there is no vengeance from our Lord at the Rapture. The vengeance of the Lord occurs at the second coming of Jesus Christ. This gives us the context of the sentence.

So now that we have the context of the sentence notice in verse 10 that our Lord is **"glorified in his saints."** The saints, which is all of the saved, are present with Him at the Second Coming. Notice also in Colossians 3.

4When Christ, *who is* our life, shall appear, then shall **ye also appear with him in glory.** (Col. 3:4)

Notice in Col 3:4 that when Christ appears, we appear with him. This is not the Rapture, for in the Rapture we do not appear with him, we are caught up to meet him. There is a big difference.

And notice what is written in the book of Jude.

14And Enoch also, the seventh from Adam,

53

The Sons of Zadok

> prophesied of these, saying, Behold, **the Lord cometh with ten thousands of his saints,**
> ¹⁵To execute judgment upon all, and to convince all that are ungodly among them of all their ungodly deeds which they have ungodly committed, and of all their hard *speeches* which ungodly sinners have spoken against him. (Jude: 14-15)

Here again you have judgement executed upon the ungodly, therefore this is a reference to the Second Advent again, and the saints are with the Lord. You are called to be a saint according to 1 Cor. 1:2 ...**called** *to be* **saints, with all that in every place call upon the name of Jesus Christ...** So, the saints are with Jesus Christ at His coming.

> ¹³To the end he may stablish your hearts unblameable in holiness before God, even our Father, at **the coming of our Lord Jesus Christ with all his saints.** (1 Thess. 3:13)

Ah, yes! That one says it all! Jesus Christ is coming with all of His saints. He does not leave the unfaithful in heaven for 1000 years. (Yes, I have heard some teach that!) All of His saints, yes, His entire Bride, is coming to earth with Him at the Second Advent of our Lord Jesus Christ.

So now that we know that we are returning to this earth with Jesus Christ, let's return to the scene in Heaven as Jesus Christ is getting ready to leave Heaven for earth.

> ¹¹And I saw heaven opened, and behold a white horse; and he that sat upon him *was* called Faithful and True, and in

The Second Coming

righteousness he doth judge and make war.

^{12}His eyes *were* as a flame of fire, and on his head *were* many crowns; and he had a name written, that no man knew, but he himself.

^{13}And he *was* clothed with a vesture dipped in blood: and his name is called The Word of God.

^{14}And the armies *which were* in heaven followed him upon white horses, clothed in fine linen, white and clean. (Rev. 19:11-14)

The streets are golden, but clear as crystal. Glistening white horses are standing on those streets. There is no darkness and thus no shadows anywhere. The angels are arrayed in white and begin to sing Alleluia and praise to the Lord. Then King Jesus stands up from the throne and walks, to the head of the great and grand army. Horses, unicorns, and saints await in eager anticipation for the order. With majesty and glory and power, Jesus strides to the front of the column. With a glance back to the throng, he shouts, *"Mount up!"*

This is where we, the army of the Lord, each get on our horse for the return to this earth. We have perfect bodies that are just like our Lord Jesus Christ. All of Heaven stands, holy hands are raised in salute as Jesus mounts up and begins to lead His army.

As He gets to the edge of Heaven, His beautiful horse rears back on its legs; with a shout from our Lord, the heavens roll back like a parchment roll. Then we launch out of the North on our horses behind our King Jesus. We are flying down through the universe and coming back to take over the earth.

The Sons of Zadok

The beautiful eyes of our Lord have now turned into the fiery eyes of the King of kings seeking vengeance on his enemies. Our Lord is now very angry. It is called wrath. He is coming in His fury, and all in his way will pay dearly with their lives.

Before the Lord returns, there is going to be a strange thing happening in the atmosphere around the earth. It is going to start raining for one month, and they are going to get a whole year's worth of rain in one month. This is called the early and latter rain in the word of God.

> ^{23}Be glad then, ye children of Zion, and rejoice in the LORD your God: for he hath given you the former rain moderately, and **he will cause to come down for you the rain, the former rain, and the latter rain in the first** *month.* (Joel 2:23)

Another thing that is going to happen is that the sky will become dark. Daytime will not be the same. It will be like a very cloudy day, but the clouds are so thick that it will be dark. Not as dark as nighttime, but dark none the less.

> ^{2}**A day of darkness and of gloominess, a day of clouds and of thick darkness,** as the morning spread upon the mountains: a great people and a strong; there hath not been ever the like, neither shall be any more after it, *even* to the years of many generations. (Joel 2:2)

The Rapture (the calling away of the Church) will happen quickly, but how quickly His return will be, I am

The Second Coming

not sure. By that, I mean how long will it actually take for us to reach earth from Heaven.

It is obvious that Jesus Christ, along with His armies could reach earth in an instant, but I am not sure this will happen. The Bible says that every eye shall see Him.

Our Lord Jesus Christ, with His armies will come down and enter the earth by Sinai, where Moses was given the law. Without touching the ground, He will then move northward to Petra. This area is known as Seir, Edom and Bozrah. It is the land where Jacob's brother Esau settled.

PETRA

^{12}I will surely assemble, O Jacob, all of thee; **I will surely gather the remnant of Israel; I will put them together as the sheep of Bozrah,** as the flock in the midst of their fold: they shall make great noise by reason of *the multitude of* men. (Mic. 2:12)

Hiding out in the caves at Petra are people, Jews, who have fled there, for their lives. They heeded the warning, and when they got the news of the abomination that was set up in the temple, they fled for their lives.

^{14}And **to the woman were given two wings of a great eagle, that she might fly into the wilderness,** into her place, where she is nourished for a time, and times, and half a time, from the face of the serpent.

^{15}And **the serpent cast out of his mouth water as a flood after the woman,** that he might cause her to be carried away of the flood.

^{16}And the earth helped the woman, and **the earth opened her mouth, and swallowed up**

The Sons of Zadok

> **the flood** which the dragon cast out of his mouth. (Rev. 12:14-16)

As Israelites flee from Jerusalem, they are given two wings of a great eagle. Is this one or two transport planes? It looks likely, but I cannot say for sure. But I do know that they are carried south to the outer desert in Edom. There in the wilderness are the caves in Petra. This is where the remnant of Israel will hide out until Jesus Christ arrives. These caves have been prepared for them by God.

Other Jews who fled for their lives, but were not living in Jerusalem, begin to arrive. As the remnant travels towards Petra, the Dragon, which is Satan, sees and attempts to kill them. He goes to Jordan and swallows up Jordan, then goes to the south and vomits it out of his belly in an attempt to drown the remnant.

> ^{23}Behold, **he drinketh up a river,** *and* hasteth not: he trusteth that he can draw up Jordan into his mouth. (Job 40:23)

As the flood waters approach the fleeing people, they see it and cry out in fear. Closer and closer the flood gets, when suddenly there is a rumbling under their feet. Just when it looked like they were doomed the earth cracks open and the water falls into the giant crevice. The remnant are saved and make it to Petra, thus uniting with the others who were there as well.

For three and half years they hide in those caves, supernaturally protected by their Lord God Jehovah. In the morning, at dawn, they go out to collect manna again. If they take too much time to collect the manna and the sun comes up, then there is the shadow of

The Second Coming

death that comes and kills them. They must get back into the caves before the shadow of death reaches them.

> ⁹We gat our bread with *the peril of* our lives because of the sword of the wilderness. (Lam. 5:9)

> ¹⁷For **the morning** *is* **to them even as the shadow of death**: if *one* know *them,* **they are** *in* **the terrors of the shadow of death.** (Job 24:17)

By now, this remnant understands that Jesus Christ is their Messiah, and the Anti-Christ is Satanic through and through. This is the remnant of Israel. The once great nation that had been a mighty kingdom under the rule of David and Solomon, is now huddled in caves in the wilderness. Their leaders had proclaimed at the trial of Jesus Christ, "His blood be upon us and our children," and my, how that has been so true.

Down through the ages, Jews have wandered throughout the earth homeless and suffering persecution. As one small testament to this fact is that there is even a plant called, *"The Wandering Jew."* The Jews have been killed, slaughtered unmercifully over and over again. Millions killed in gas chambers under Hitler. To study the history of Israel is to see that the word of God is true.

How many Jews are left, huddled in the caves, that make up this remnant? I do not know, but it is not many. Could it be 700? or 7000? Not over 10,000 would be my liberal guess.

The time of the end has now arrived. Their suffering and deliverance by the Messiah is beginning. In the

The Sons of Zadok

caves they do not see the sky, but out of the North comes a throng of people being led by the King of kings and Lord of lords. The Bible says that,

⁷Behold, he cometh with clouds; and **every eye shall see him**, and they *also* which pierced him: and all kindreds of the earth shall wail because of him. Even so, Amen. (Rev. 1:7)

To the rest of the world it could go something like this: *Look! Up in the sky! It's a bird, it's a plane, it's... it's... superm... it's the Lord Jesus Christ! Oh no!*

The horses are white. The soldiers are dressed in white. Their leader is on a white horse, and He is also dressed in white. At first it looks like a massive, ever-growing larger cloud, but then it can be seen that it is a multitude of beings. As the "cloud" gets closer it can be seen they are people riding on horses, and they are coming ever closer to the earth.

If every eye shall see Him, then perhaps it takes 24 hours for the Lord and His army to land. Yes, it could be that all the earth sees the Lord and His army coming through their digital devices: such as phones, tablets and computers. But there is a likelihood that electricity will be gone by the end of the Tribulation. So, whether it is one revolution of the earth, (and you flat-earthers are nuts!) or if all see what's coming by way of wifi, either way the whole earth sees Him coming in the clouds with great glory.

And when it says great glory, it shows that there is shining of bright white light that emanates from this oncoming band of soldiers that is being led by the King of the universe. Closer and closer, brighter and brighter

The Second Coming

it gets. With it comes a dread and ominous feeling that those upon the earth who have taken the mark of the beast are in for trouble and fiery indignation.

The Lord has been patient for six thousand years. He has waited for the day of vengeance and now that time has arrived. He has allowed His name being used as a cuss word. He has allowed blasphemous movies, stories, and religious ceremonies to take place daily. He has allowed people to claim they eat Him and cast the refuse out in the drought. He has allowed puny, mortal man to vaunt himself and claim to be stronger and to be more righteous than God Himself. Patiently through the millennia He has allowed it, all the while longing for people to repent.

> [9]The Lord is not slack concerning his promise, as some men count slackness; but is **longsuffering to us-ward, not willing that any should perish,** but that all should come to repentance. (2 Pet. 3:9)

His patience is now over. His longsuffering towards rebellious man is now over. Vengeance, fury, wrath, anger, rage are all words that describe the Lord Jesus Christ at this time. Of course, that brings a thought to my mind. If He is God, then why does He not just speak and obliterate them all? He obviously has the power to do that. So why doesn't He just get it over with?

It's because He now wants the pleasure of personally killing and bringing judgement upon those who vaunted themselves against him. That is something to think about! The Lord is looking forward to personally inflicting vengeance and judgement upon those who

The Sons of Zadok

have rebelled against Him. And this is now the time that He has been waiting for.

Down, down He comes through the air on His white horse. Behind Him are millions of saints upon white horses as well. But this first battle is His, all His. He doesn't want any help, nor does He need any help. He is attacking, destroying, and stomping people in His furious rage and enjoys doing it. His first battle is in Seir, which is also known as Edom as well as Bozrah. It is south east of the Dead Sea.

Huddled in the caves, the people hear something strange. Something that they have never heard before. It is like the sound of many waters. Or is it the sound of thunder? It is not the sound of horse hooves beating the ground because the Lord and His army are not on the ground but flying over head.

The remnant of emaciated, weak Jews cautiously peer out from the caves. Looking up into the small bit of sky they see a miracle. Deliverance! Their Messiah has returned. The first brave souls that ventured out begin to shout for joy, and tears run down their cheeks. They then shout to the rest, *"Come see! It's Jesus, Messiah! We are saved!"* Others begin to venture out to see the sight, and they, too, begin to shout and praise the Lord. Others fall on their knees in tears and worship the Lord with shouts of praise to the Lamb of God. With arms out stretched they bow with their faces to the ground. Messiah has returned! Oh, Happy day!!

Not far away in Bozrah is an army of wicked people. They have tried to kill off the remnant of the Jews, but the Lord has not let them. Now it is time for the Lord

The Second Coming

to kill them off. As He lands, He dismounts His beautiful white steed and begins to destroy those who are against Him.

¹Who *is* this that **cometh from Edom**, with dyed garments from Bozrah? this *that is* glorious in his apparel, travelling in the greatness of his strength? I that speak in righteousness, mighty to save.

²Wherefore *art thou* red in thine apparel, and thy garments like him that treadeth in the winefat?

³I have trodden the winepress alone; and of the people *there was* none with me: for I will tread them in mine anger, and trample them in my fury; and their blood shall be sprinkled upon my garments, and I will stain all my raiment.

⁴For the day of vengeance *is* in mine heart, and the year of my redeemed is come.

⁵And I looked, and *there was* none to help; and I wondered that *there was* none to uphold: therefore mine own arm brought salvation unto me; and my fury, it upheld me.

⁶And **I will tread down the people in mine anger, and make them drunk in my fury**, and I will bring down their strength to the earth. (Isa. 63:1-6)

As Jesus Christ furiously stomps them, blood splatters upon His beautiful white garments. Red blotches on the white robe increase as the base of his robe turns full red as it is now dripping with the blood

The Sons of Zadok

of the wicked slain. They are made drunk with the fury of the Lord. Staggering, stumbling, falling, puking, and then getting their heads smashed in as the Lord stomps on them, all the while laughing in His furious rage.

As He died alone on Calvary, so too now he destroys them alone in the fields of blood south of the Dead Sea in Edom. Some try to run, but He is faster. They do not escape, for He sees all. As we, the saints of His army look on, we cheer and shout praise to the Lord God Almighty. Hallelujah to the Lamb of God! He is the true Lord God and this is the time of his vengeance and proof of who He truly is.

The remnant of the Jews at Petra are delivered, and the wicked armies of the Anti-Christ that were stationed there are destroyed. This is the first victory that takes place when our Lord returns to take what is rightfully his. He created it all, and he is now taking over the earth. All hail the power of our Lord Jesus Christ!

Their Messiah has finally returned as promised.

> [22]Behold, he shall come up and fly as the eagle, and spread his wings over Bozrah: and at that day shall **the heart of the mighty men of Edom be as the heart of a woman in her pangs.** (Jer. 49:22)

> [12]But I will send a fire upon Teman, which shall devour the palaces of Bozrah. (Amos 1:12)

From Petra, He leaves and heads north on the King's Highway: He crosses the Jordan River where John the Baptist baptized Him 2000 years earlier. From there, He heads due west to take over Jerusalem. He is flying, and so are we on our white horses.

The Second Coming

THE CAPTURE OF JERUSALEM

The amount of information in the word of God for this event is quite large, and since this book is not primarily about this event, I am going to limit the amount of scripture and the description of this event.

⁴For thus hath the LORD spoken unto me, Like as the lion and the young lion roaring on his prey, when a multitude of shepherds is called forth against him, *he* will not be afraid of their voice, nor abase himself for the noise of them: so shall the LORD of hosts come down to fight for mount Zion, and for the hill thereof.

⁵**As birds flying**, so will the LORD of hosts defend Jerusalem; defending also he will deliver *it; and* **passing over** he will preserve it. (Isa. 31:4-5)

So as the Lord and His army cross the Jordan River, He comes to Jerusalem. Here the devil has set himself up as God in the house of God with the image of the beast. This is also described in the word of God as the "**...abomination of desolation**" (Matt. 24:15). This is the zenith of blasphemy, and the Lord is furious. Jerusalem is the city of the great King, and that great King is the Lord Jesus Christ. He has now come to take it back. As He leads His army, you must keep in mind that they are not on the ground for Isa. 31:5 says, "**...as birds flying...**".

As He approaches the city, people stand to resist Him. This is when He speaks, and a blast goes out of His mouth that literally melts those in front of Him.

The Sons of Zadok

> ⁸And then shall that Wicked be revealed, whom the Lord shall **consume with the spirit of his mouth, and shall destroy with the brightness of his coming:** (2 Thess. 2:8)
>
> ¹²And this shall be the plague wherewith the LORD will smite all the people that have fought against Jerusalem; **Their flesh shall consume away while they stand upon their feet, and their eyes shall consume away in their holes, and their tongue shall consume away in their mouth.** (Zech. 14:12)

The power and heat of the blast that is projected out of our Lord's mouth is so strong that the people literally melt like wax in a fire. It is at this time that the Anti-Christ is consumed with the spirit of the Lord's mouth and destroyed with the brightness of His coming.

I find it amazing, yet there is nothing new under the sun. In the movies it is a common sight that when super heroes fight, they will often be portrayed with fire or a stream of "energy" coming out of their mouths or eyes in the midst of battles.

Even in Job 41, Leviathan, is described as being a fire-breathing dragon. But he is an imperfect counterfeit of the true, for Jesus Christ has all power in Heaven and earth. He is the One who has the supreme power to destroy those whom He desires to destroy, and it is not hard for Him to destroy them. The Lord Jesus Christ is their Creator.

The following, fairly-detailed description of the attack and conquering of Jerusalem at the Second Coming of Christ is found in the second chapter of Joel. I am going to limit the rest of the description of this battle to

The Second Coming

the description found in Joel. One of the reasons is that in Joel, you will be given details about what you and I will be doing in this battle.

The deliverance of Petra was done solely by our Lord Jesus Christ, but in this battle we have a part. And it really is an amazing description that is given here in the book of Joel. Read the following slowly and picture yourself in this battle, for if you are born again, then you will be there.

In Joel 2:1 it is "...the day of the LORD..." which is clearly the second advent of our Lord Jesus Christ.

> ^{1}Blow ye the trumpet in Zion, and sound an alarm in my holy mountain: let all the inhabitants of the land tremble: for **the day of the LORD cometh**, for *it is* nigh at hand;
>
> ^{2}A day of darkness and of gloominess, a day of clouds and of thick darkness, as the morning spread upon the mountains: **a great people and a strong; there hath not been ever the like**, neither shall be any more after it, *even* to the years of many generations.
>
> ^{3}A fire devoureth before them; and behind them a flame burneth: the land *is* as the garden of Eden before them, and behind them a desolate wilderness; yea, and nothing shall escape them.
>
> ^{4}The appearance of them *is* as the appearance of **horses; and as horsemen**, so shall they run.
>
> ^{5}Like the noise of chariots on the tops of mountains shall they leap, like the noise of a flame of fire that devoureth the stubble, as a

67

The Sons of Zadok

strong people set in battle array.

⁶Before their face the people shall be much pained: **all faces shall gather blackness.**

⁷They shall run like mighty men; they shall climb the wall like men of war; and they shall march every one on his ways, and they shall not break their ranks:

⁸Neither shall one thrust another; they shall walk every one in his path: and *when* **they fall upon the sword, they shall not be wounded.**

⁹They shall run to and fro in the city; they shall run upon the wall, they shall climb up upon the houses; **they shall enter in at the windows like a thief.**

¹⁰The earth shall quake before them; the heavens shall tremble: the sun and the moon shall be dark, and the stars shall withdraw their shining:

¹¹And the LORD shall utter his voice before **his army:** for his camp *is* very great: for *he is* strong that executeth his word: for the day of the LORD *is* great and very terrible; and who can abide it? (Joel 2:1-10)

¹⁶Gather the people, sanctify the congregation, assemble the elders, gather the children, and those that suck the breasts: **let the bridegroom go forth of his chamber, and the bride out of her closet.** (Joel 2:16)

"As birds flying," we circle over Jerusalem and then land. Soldiers, people, and all who have taken the mark of the beast are there to fight us.

The Second Coming

What is interesting to me is a simple little statement that is mentioned in Joel which is this:

> [8] Neither shall one thrust another; they shall walk every one in his path: and **when they fall upon the sword, they shall not be wounded.** (Joel 2:8)

We are going to have bodies just like Jesus Christ.

> [21] **Who shall change our vile body, that it may be fashioned like unto his glorious body,** according to the working whereby he is able even to subdue all things unto himself. (Phil. 3:21)

Not only will we have bodies just like the risen Jesus Christ, but we are going to have the same mentality as our Lord. This is our Lord's rightful day to return with vengeance. And the Lord will possess a fury which is such that He will laugh and mock those whom He is destroying. It is called vengeance. Not merely judgment, but vengeance. There is a difference. Vengeance has anger associated with it. Combined with this anger is personal satisfaction that where you were wronged, you are now allowed and able to inflict the punishment that is due. He who laughs last, laughs best!

So, here we are, the born again saints of our Lord Jesus Christ. We are the bride of Christ, also known as the Church. We are fighting in this battle as well, and it is a great battle to fight for we will not lose and we cannot die.

So my question is this: if we cannot die, and we will not break our ranks, and we have bodies just like our Lord, then why do we fall upon our sword? "**...when they fall upon the sword...**" (Joel 2:8) We certainly will

The Sons of Zadok

not trip, for gravity is irrelevant to us anyway. But if the Lord is vexing and mocking His enemies and laughing at their calamity, then we are likely to have the same attitude.

So, as we encounter soldiers who are trying to kill us, we will let them stick us with their sword and then laugh as they realize we are immortal. Or, since it says, "fall upon," we will mock them by falling upon a sword in front of them and then get up unharmed right before their faces. As they realize their doom, we will laugh, mock, and then kill them. This is our day. This is our time. He who laughs last, laughs best. Aren't you glad you're saved?!

Dear reader, perhaps you are having a hard time. Maybe people are using you, or you are getting abused at work or home, and you are getting discouraged. Remember, your day is coming. If you are saved, then you are going to fight in this battle and win.

BATTLE AT MEGIDDO

North of Jerusalem is a place which is called the valley of Megiddo. It is the sight of the battle of Armageddon. This is the last battle in the Lord's campaign to take over the earth, and this is the bloodiest of them all. Like the battle in Petra, so the Lord too fights this one all by Himself.

As the Lord enters the valley and engages the armies of the devil, it becomes apparent that those earthly armies are in very serious trouble. For as they use their weapons against the Lord, they suddenly find out that

The Second Coming

their weapons have no power whatsoever against the Lord and His army.

^{20}And the winepress was trodden without the city, and **blood came out of the winepress, even unto the horse bridles**, by the space of a thousand *and* six hundred furlongs. (Rev. 14:20)

The Lord is now riding His horse with its feet on the ground. And with each step, wicked enemy fighters are being trampled under foot of His horse. The Bible likens it to a wine press, but the people are the grapes that are being crushed by the horse hooves which are spurred on by the wrath of almighty God. This is where the saying, "the grapes of wrath" comes from. This is the famous battle of Armageddon. It is the battle where the term, "we stomped them" comes from. In this battle the enemy will literally be stomped to death. Blood begins to flow. A little at first and then more and more it begins to fill the valley.

As the enemy sees he is powerless to stop the onslaught of the battle, many of them begin to cry out for mercy. Others openly blaspheme and curse at Him in open rebellion. The Lord, in His fury begins to laugh at them all. He begins to mock them as they cry or curse at Him. Yes, the *"meek and lowly Galilean"* is now mocking and laughing at those He is killing.

^{24}Because I have called, and ye refused; I have stretched out my hand, and no man regarded;

^{25}But ye have set at nought all my counsel, and would none of my reproof:

^{26}**I also will laugh at your calamity; I will**

The Sons of Zadok

>mock when your fear cometh;
>²⁷When your fear cometh as desolation, and your destruction cometh as a whirlwind; when distress and anguish cometh upon you. (Prov. 1:24-27)
>²The kings of the earth set themselves, and the rulers take counsel together, against the LORD, and against his anointed, *saying*,
>³Let us break their bands asunder, and cast away their cords from us.
>**⁴He that sitteth in the heavens shall laugh: the Lord shall have them in derision.**
>**⁵Then shall he speak unto them in his wrath, and vex them in his sore displeasure.**
>⁹Thou shalt break them with a rod of iron; thou shalt **dash them in pieces** like a potter's vessel. (Psa. 2:2-5; 9)

The Lord Jesus Christ is now vexing them in His anger like a cat with a mouse. He is purposefully agitating them. As they plead and beg for mercy, or curse and shake their clenched fist in His face, He laughs and puts a horses hoof right down on a knee, or a shoulder as a scream of pain splits the air. Then another stomp on the head, and they are done. With that, a loud victory laugh peals out from the Lord Jesus Christ as He rides on into the sea of bodies. People who now are trying to flee have nowhere to go, for it is a valley. Not only that, but the attackers are supernatural.

Then in the middle of it all, the Lord gets off His horse and begins to stomp the people with His own bare feet. As they plead for mercy, He mocks them. With His eyes

The Second Coming

like fire, He is furious at these wicked people. Yes, He hates them and is now enjoying destroying them personally. This is the other side of the God of love.

Yes, God is love, for the Bible does state that He is. But it also states that our "**...our God is a consuming fire**" (Heb. 12:29) and "**...he that believeth not the Son shall not see life; but the wrath of God abideth on him**" (Jn 3:36). On this day the wrath of God is going to be exercised on the heathen. Can you imagine the bloody, yet glorious sight?

A soldier, who minutes earlier thought he was so tough with the heart of a lion, has now turned into a fearful wretch with full realization he has no chance of victory. His heart is said to become the, "**...heart of a woman**" (Jer. 48:41). With anguish on his face and fear in his voice, the joints of his knees give out as he trembles for the first time in his life:

"L..L..Lord Jesus, I..I'm so sorry. Please, please I beg of you to forgive me. Oh God, I know I've done wrong. Dear Lord, I..."

The Lord Jesus Christ begins to vex him as He knocks the sinner to the bloody mud with a back hand. A loud *"Ha Ha Ha"* goes out of the Lord's mouth. Sarcastically Jesus says, *"Oh, I fully know you have done wrong. How do you like being on all fours? Finally, you have gotten on your knees."* Then the Lord leans over and says in his ear, *"But it's too late!"* And with that, He puts a foot down on his back that flattens him out, and the other foot slams on his head and crushes his skull in.

Blood sprinkles and stains the raiment of the Lord as He moves onward through the people. Back up on his

The Sons of Zadok

horse, He gallops alone in the middle of the valley, stomping the people.

> ³I have trodden the winepress alone; and of the people *there was* none with me... (Isa. 63:3)

Ah, yes! The personal satisfaction of proper vengeance realized. It has taken over 6000 years to arrive, but at last the scripture is fulfilled,

> ¹⁹Dearly beloved, avenge not yourselves, but *rather* give place unto wrath: for it is written, **Vengeance *is* mine; I will repay, saith the Lord.** (Rom. 12:19)

The King of glory has returned and captured His kingdom. The Tribulation is now over, and the battles are done. Our Lord Jesus Christ is the conquering King and victory is His.

In the wake of the Tribulation and final battles, the earth is in shambles. Wars, pestilences, earthquakes, volcanoes, heat, have taken their toll. Dead fish in the ocean, destroyed buildings, broken sewers, and garbage are everywhere. Dead bodies lie rotting all over the world, with animals gorging them until they can eat no more. Over in Megiddo the stench is horrible.

> ⁹And they that dwell in the cities of Israel shall go forth, and shall set on fire and burn the weapons, both the shields and the bucklers, the bows and the arrows, and the handstaves, and the spears, and **they shall burn them with fire seven years:**
>
> ¹⁰So that they shall take no wood out of the field, neither cut down *any* out of the forests;

The Second Coming

for they shall burn the weapons with fire: and they shall spoil those that spoiled them, and rob those that robbed them, saith the Lord GOD.

^{11}And it shall come to pass in that day, *that* I will give unto Gog a place there of graves in Israel, the valley of the passengers on the east of the sea: and **it shall stop the *noses* of the passengers:** and there shall they bury Gog and all his multitude: and they shall call *it* The valley of Hamongog.

^{12}And **seven months shall the house of Israel be burying of them, that they may cleanse the land.**

^{13}Yea, all the people of the land shall bury *them*; and **it shall be to them a renown** the day that I shall be glorified, saith the Lord GOD. (Ezek. 39:9-13)

It will take seven months to bury the slain at Megiddo:

^{17}And I saw an angel standing in the sun; and he cried with a loud voice, saying to all the fowls that fly in the midst of heaven, Come and gather yourselves together unto the supper of the great God;

^{18}That ye may eat the flesh of kings, and the flesh of captains, and the flesh of mighty men, and the flesh of horses, and of them that sit on them, and the flesh of all *men, both* free and bond, both small and great. (Rev. 19:17-18)

The Sons of Zadok

Israel shall bury them. Not the Gentiles, but the house of Israel. It is a great day for Israel. A long awaited day. The day that many had said would never come, or that it was only a dream. What day is that? The millennial day of the Lord. The 1000 year reign of the Lord Jesus Christ.

After Megiddo, the Lord returns triumphantly to Jerusalem. Bodies smolder in the streets as smoke ascends from their charred remains. Buildings are broken down and in shambles. A very small amount of people had remained in the city of Jerusalem. They now begin to venture out to see what is left of the city. Some have heard that The Lord Jesus Christ has taken over the city, as well as the world.

To those that remain who have taken the mark of the Beast, this is very bad news. It means they are doomed and will be cast into outer darkness where there shall be weeping, wailing, and gnashing of teeth. To the *very few* that remain in the city who have not taken the mark, this is very great news, for it means they are safe. It also means they can eat. No doubt they are skin and bones, as well as very, very weak.

There will not be many in the city who have not taken the mark. It will be out in the wilds that the people who refused to take the mark are inhabiting. They have run for their lives to escape death for not taking the mark while under the rule Anti-Christ. They couldn't buy or sell, so they ran to live off whatever they could find to eat.

Word travels throughout the world quickly that the Lord Jesus Christ has returned, and those without the mark are now safe. For many, it will be tears of joy.

The Second Coming

Shouting and happiness will break forth into singing as even nature itself rejoices that the King of Glory has returned.

Back in Jerusalem, King Jesus walks triumphantly into His temple, sits down on the throne and the Millennium begins. There is much clean up to do, as well as cleansing the temple. But the King has returned and taken over what is rightfully His. Hallelujah!!!

The Sons of Zadok

Chapter 3

Establishment of the Kingdom

The King, the Lord Jesus Christ, enters Jerusalem through the eastern gate. Sometime in or after the first month, the sky that had been so dark with clouds begins to brighten up. As the clouds part, it becomes much, much brighter, yet the sun is not burning the people or things on the ground.

^{25}And there shall be upon every high mountain, and upon every high hill, rivers *and* streams of waters in the day of the great slaughter, when the towers fall. ^{26}Moreover **the light of the moon shall be as the light of the sun, and the light of the sun shall be sevenfold, as the light of seven days,** in the day that the LORD bindeth up the breach of his people, and healeth the stroke of their wound. (Isa. 30:25-26)

The sun will become seven times brighter than it is now. Yet, there will be people in the Millennium who

The Sons of Zadok

have survived the Tribulation, and they will have mortal bodies like you and I do right now. They will still be living in Adamic, corrupt bodies. So with the sun shining seven times brighter, there must be a change in the light.

This is an assumption, but in the body that I have right now, if I stood out in the sun that was seven times brighter, I wouldn't be able to open my eyes and probably would be covering them with my hands.

Not only that, but my skin would burn in a matter of seconds or maybe a minute. Right now my skin burns in a matter of 20 to 30 minutes. If my skin *burns* in 21 minutes and you divided that by 7 then my skin would burn in three minutes. With the sun seven times brighter, the moon also is seven times brighter. The light of a full moon in the Millennium is the same brightness as the daytime is now.

So things begin to change drastically on this earth in the first part of the Millennium. Our Lord Jesus Christ is making things right and as they were intended to be. It will be very close to how the earth was in the Garden of Eden.

The animals will be vegetarians.

> ^{7}**And the cow and the bear shall feed; their young ones shall lie down together: and the lion shall eat straw like the ox.**
>
> ^{8}**And the sucking child shall play on the hole of the asp, and the weaned child shall put his hand on the cockatrice' den.** (Isa. 11:7-8)
>
> ^{25}**The wolf and the lamb shall feed together, and the lion shall eat straw like the bullock:** and dust *shall be* the serpent's meat. They

The Set Up of The Millennium

shall not hurt nor destroy in all my holy mountain, saith the LORD. (Isa. 65:25)

So the curse that was placed upon nature in Genesis 3 will be removed. Roses will not have thorns and the ground will not bring forth thorns and thistles any more. The poisonous snakes, such as the Cockatrice, will no longer be poisonous. A child will be able to play with them. Obviously the fear and enmity between man and nature is removed. The animals will not fear man, and man will not fear the animals. Having a lion or an eagle as a pet will be a reality. Actually the animals will be around in such a way that they will all seem like pets. If there will ever be a time when man is one with nature, then this will be that time.

By the way, in the Garden of Eden Adam and Eve did not eat vegetables. They ate of the fruit of the trees. When they picked the fruit of the trees, they never had to bend over to pick the fruit. In the Millennium it is likely to be like that once again, but this is an assumption on my part. I do know that the sacrifices will be in operation and the priests will eat meat from the sacrifices. So while many things in the Millennium will be similar to the Garden of Eden, it will not be exactly the same.

The harvesting in the Millennium will be amazing. There will be no bad weather, no weeds, no bugs nor mold to destroy the crops. With the curse lifted and the sun shining, the crops will bring forth abundantly. The plowers will be coming along right behind the reapers.

[13] Behold, the days come, saith the LORD,
> that **the plowman shall overtake the reaper,
> and the treader of grapes him that soweth**

The Sons of Zadok

seed; and the mountains shall drop sweet wine, and all the hills shall melt. (Amos 9:13)

The curse being lifted is a good thing, and it is likely that women will have much easier childbirth. Along with that, there will be very little sickness, and as it says in Ezekiel 47:12 "...**the leaf thereof for medicine.**" Where the waters flow out from under the temple, the trees grow, and the leaves of the trees are used for medicine. And there is no doubt about that medicine working. So the population will literally explode in numbers, which is a good thing.

You see, the Lord Jesus Christ loves people. He died to save them. During the Millennium there is going to be a very, very great number of people on this earth. By the time the thousand years is finished, there will be many, many billions of people. It would not surprise me if by the end of the Millennium there is close to one trillion people on this earth. And even if that is true, there will be no food shortages. It will be a time of great joy, peace and safety on this earth.

Another thing that will take place in the beginning of the Millennium is that the land will be rearranged according to how the Lord wants it. Have you ever wondered about the following verse? It seems kind of strange.

> [21] Jesus answered and said unto them, Verily I say unto you, If ye have faith, and doubt not, ye shall not only do this *which is done* to the fig tree, but also if **ye shall say unto this mountain, Be thou removed, and be thou cast into the sea; it shall be done.** (Matt. 21:21)

Doesn't that seem a bit strange? It does to me.

The Set Up of The Millennium

Unless in the Millennium we get to landscape the earth. After all, don't you enjoy landscaping your front and back yard? Don't you enjoy having a garden? Some of you may not, but most people really do enjoy planting and arranging a garden. After all, life started in a garden.

Maybe you live in an apartment and can't have a garden, but there is a chance that you have some plants to care for in your apartment or on a patio. The desire to plant and grow things is in us. And for those of you who do not have a "green thumb," you will be able to grow whatever you want, and it will flourish.

> [4] **Every valley shall be exalted, and every mountain and hill shall be made low: and the crooked shall be made straight, and the rough places plain:**
>
> [5] And the glory of the LORD shall be revealed, and all flesh shall see it together: for the mouth of the LORD hath spoken *it*. (Isa. 40:4-5)

According to verse 4, then the earth is going to be leveled out. Will it all be a flat plain? I doubt it, but that is my opinion. I would guess it will be more like gently rolling hills with streams running between them. There will be no crooked places, and I have seen some crooked places! In Arizona there are some crooked places, and steep canyons, such as the Grand Canyon.

I grew up in the Sierra Nevada Mountains at 4000 feet elevation. I backpacked over "Old Sammy" which was over 11,000 feet high. On one side of the ridge the waters flowed down to the Bay area of California and into the Pacific Ocean. On the other side of the ridge, the waters flowed down to the Colorado River and into

The Sons of Zadok

the Gulf of Baja in Mexico. It was a high, crooked area with steep cliffs. One day though, those mountains are going to be flattened out and the valleys are going to be exalted. Instead of barren, gray granite rocks, it will become a beautiful flowering place of crops, people and prosperity.

What if God was to come up to you and give you a portion of the earth and say, *"This is for you to make it however you want it."* You could move mountains and valleys. You could plant and grow things as well as raise animals, and probably the animals would not need fences to stay around. Wouldn't that be something?

This Millennial time is said to be a regeneration. The earth, in a way, is going to be born again when Jesus Christ resides on this planet. And as He resides here, not only will the land, plants and animals be changed greatly for the better, but the population will be dealt with as well.

The first major dealing is going to be the Judgement of Nations. (The Christians judgement will be over having taken place at the Judgement seat of Christ.) The Lord is going to settle some accounts as well as complete the first resurrection. By the end of the Judgement of Nations, all who are saved from Genesis to the start of the Millennium will be resurrected.

> [1] And I saw an angel come down from heaven, having the key of the bottomless pit and a great chain in his hand.
>
> [2] And he laid hold on the dragon, that old serpent, which is the Devil, and Satan, and bound him a thousand years,
>
> [3] And cast him into the bottomless pit, and

The Set Up of The Millennium

> shut him up, and set a seal upon him, that he should deceive the nations no more, till the thousand years should be fulfilled: and after that he must be loosed a little season.
>
> [4]And I saw thrones, and they sat upon them, and judgment was given unto them: and *I saw* the souls of them that were beheaded for the witness of Jesus, and for the word of God, and which had not worshipped the beast, neither his image, neither had received *his* mark upon their foreheads, or in their hands; and they lived and reigned with Christ a thousand years.
>
> [5]But the rest of the dead lived not again until the thousand years were finished. **This is the first resurrection.** (Rev. 20:1-5)

At the start of the Millennium, the satanic trinity is dealt with and cast into the bottomless pit. Amen! One thousand years of no satanic influence on this earth.

There's an amazing conversation recorded in the word of God. It is a conversation that takes place when Lucifer enters Hell. It really is amazing, all that is found in the word of God, isn't it!

> [9]Hell from beneath is moved for thee to meet *thee* at thy coming: it stirreth up the dead for thee, *even* all the chief ones of the earth; it hath raised up from their thrones all the kings of the nations.
>
> [10]All they shall speak and say unto thee, **Art thou also become weak as we?** art thou become like unto us?
>
> [11]Thy pomp is brought down to the grave,

The Sons of Zadok

and the noise of thy viols: the worm is spread under thee, and the worms cover thee.

^{12}**How art thou fallen from heaven, O Lucifer, son of the morning!** *how* **art thou cut down to the ground, which didst weaken the nations!**

^{13}For thou hast said in thine heart, I will ascend into heaven, I will exalt my throne above the stars of God: I will sit also upon the mount of the congregation, in the sides of the north:

^{14}I will ascend above the heights of the clouds; I will be like the most High.

^{15}**Yet thou shalt be brought down to hell, to the sides of the pit.** (Isa. 14:9-15)

There is a note that must be made here. In verse 12 your King James 1611 Bible reads, "**O Lucifer, son of the morning!**" This is the only place where the name "Lucifer" is mentioned. But the modern versions remove the name of Lucifer and change it to a blasphemous reading. They remove all reference to this being Lucifer and thus the Devil, and change it to a title given to our Lord Jesus Christ. It is this verse they change that shows these new versions are corrupt and inspired by Satan himself!!

In the New International Version of 1984 it reads, "**O morning star, son of the dawn!**" The name of Lucifer is removed so the reader doesn't know who is being talked about, and then one of the names for Jesus Christ is inserted for the name of Lucifer, that being "**morning star.**"

King James 1611 Bible reads:

^{16}I Jesus have sent mine angel to testify unto

The Set Up of The Millennium

you these things in the churches. I am the root and the offspring of David, *and* **the bright and morning star.** (Rev. 22:16)

"Morning star" is a name for Jesus Christ and the New International Version uses one of our Lord's names in place of the name Lucifer. The NIV is a Satanic inspired, godless, piece of trash. If you love Jesus Christ and are using an NIV, you need to throw it out and get yourself a King James 1611 Bible.

King James 1611 reads:
^{19}We have also a more sure word of prophecy; whereunto ye do well that ye take heed, as unto a light that shineth in a dark place, until the day dawn, and **the day star** arise in your hearts: (2 Pet. 1:19)

The English Standard Version reads *"Day Star"* with the name of Lucifer missing.

> Isa. 14:12 ¶ "How you are fallen from heaven, O Day Star, 'son of Dawn! How you are cut down to the ground, you who laid the nations low!

Todays English version reads *"morning star."* With Lucifer missing.

> Is. 14:12 King of Babylon, bright morning star, you have fallen from heaven! In the past you conquered nations, but now you have been thrown to the ground.

New American Standard Version, *"day star."* With Lucifer missing.

> Is. 14:12 "How you have fallen from heaven, O star of the morning, son of the dawn! You have been cut down to the earth, You who have weakened the nations!

God's Word translation reads, *"morning star."* Lucifer

The Sons of Zadok

missing.

> Is. 14:12 ¶ How you have fallen from heaven, you morning star, son of the dawn! How you have been cut down to the ground, you conqueror of nations!

If you do not read from a King James 1611 in English, you are reading from a Satanically-inspired, corrupt piece of trash that isn't worth the match it would take to burn it!!! Those four versions that I just quoted from are *blaspheming the Lord Jesus Christ* by taking a name for Jesus Christ and inserting it into the text for Lucifer. If that is not enough for you to throw it out and get you a King James 1611 Bible, you are not right with God! To reject the light you just got is to lose rewards at the judgement seat of Christ.

It is interesting that the new versions would corrupt that verse. It shows that they are satanically-led by messing with that verse. There is a spirit that does not want you to know what the word of God says is going to happen to Lucifer at the end of the Tribulation. It is like the fake news and the rewriting of history. If the information is not available, then we can continue on in our own reality.

No, it doesn't work that way. Your *"reality"* is a lie; one day the Lord Jesus Christ is coming back, and the truth is going to be made known. The truth is, the satanic trinity is going to the bottomless pit at the end of the Tribulation. Then at the White Throne Judgement he is going to be thrown into the Lake of Fire after...after...after he confesses that Jesus is Lord to the glory of God the Father. Amen and Amen!!!

Those who took the mark of the beast are going to be dealt with, as well as those who did not take the mark of the beast.

The Set Up of The Millennium

⁹And the third angel followed them, saying with a loud voice, **If any man worship the beast and his image, and receive *his* mark in his forehead, or in his hand,**

¹⁰The same shall drink of the wine of the wrath of God, which is poured out without mixture into the cup of his indignation; and he **shall be tormented with fire and brimstone in the presence of the holy angels, and in the presence of the Lamb:**

¹¹**And the smoke of their torment ascendeth up for ever and ever: and they have no rest day nor night, who worship the beast and his image, and whosoever receiveth the mark of his name.** (Rev. 14:9-11)

At this judgement of nations people are judged for how they treated the Jew during the Tribulation.

³⁵For I was an hungred, and ye gave me meat: I was thirsty, and ye gave me drink: I was a stranger, and ye took me in:

³⁶Naked, and ye clothed me: I was sick, and ye visited me: I was in prison, and ye came unto me.

³⁷Then shall the righteous answer him, saying, Lord, when saw we thee an hungred, and fed *thee*? or thirsty, and gave *thee* drink?

³⁸When saw we thee a stranger, and took *thee* in? or naked, and clothed *thee*?

³⁹Or when saw we thee sick, or in prison, and came unto thee?

⁴⁰And the King shall answer and say unto them, Verily I say unto you, **Inasmuch as ye**

The Sons of Zadok

have done *it* unto one of the least of these my brethren, ye have done *it* unto me. (Matt. 25:35-40)

As a Christian, you have had a part in the first resurrection. You will have gone to Heaven at death, or you will have met the Lord in the air with all of the saved at the Rapture. Either way you are safe and have part in the first resurrection.

You will notice as well that in Revelation 20:4, there are thrones and judgment is given unto those sitting on those thrones. Who that is, I am not sure. It might be you and me, but I believe our judging will take place at the Great White Throne Judgement.

[2] Do ye not know that **the saints shall judge the world?** and if the world shall be judged by you, are ye unworthy to judge the smallest matters?

[3] Know ye not that **we shall judge angels?** how much more things that pertain to this life? (1Cor. 6:2-3)

Whether it is at the start of the Millennium, or at the Great White Throne Judgment, or both, if you are saved, then you are going to judge the world and angels. That really is an amazing thought! In this mortal life the Christian is to serve the Lord Jesus Christ and to suffer with Him, but there is a day coming when that will all be over. The faithful Christian will judge and reign with the Lord Jesus Christ. Of course, I was careful to say *"faithful."* For those born again Christians who were not faithful, it is a different story.

Before I say more, let me qualify that statement. Can we all do better? Yes! Have we all had times where we

The Set Up of The Millennium

let the Lord down? Yes! But as we examine it more in the next chapters, remember this: *the ones that try*, gain. (Luke 19). The majority of Christians are not *trying* to do their best. Jesus Christ is not first in their hearts and life. They have not picked up their cross. They are not faithful.

Dear Christian, will you, or are you, *trying* to do your best? It is not a matter of how much or the size of your service/ministry. It is this: are you trying to be faithful? If you are, then you will be judging and reigning with our Lord Jesus Christ. If not...well, we will see as we get into it.

The Sons of Zadok

Chapter 4

The Sons of Zadok

What Will You Do for 1000 Years?

The following verses, though a lengthy passage, are the origin and inspiration for this sermon and book.

¹Then he brought me back the way of the gate of the outward sanctuary which looketh toward the east; and it *was* shut.

²Then said the LORD unto me; This gate shall be shut, it shall not be opened, and no man shall enter in by it; because the LORD, the God of Israel, hath entered in by it, therefore it shall be shut.

³*It is* for the prince; the prince, he shall sit in it to eat bread before the LORD; he shall enter by the way of the porch of *that* gate, and shall go out by the way of the same.

⁴Then brought he me the way of the north gate before the house: and I looked, and,

behold, the glory of the LORD filled the house of the LORD: and I fell upon my face.

⁵And the LORD said unto me, Son of man, mark well, and behold with thine eyes, and hear with thine ears all that I say unto thee concerning all the ordinances of the house of the LORD, and all the laws thereof; and mark well the entering in of the house, with every going forth of the sanctuary.

⁶And thou shalt say to the rebellious, *even* to the house of Israel, Thus saith the Lord GOD; O ye house of Israel, let it suffice you of all your abominations,

⁷In that ye have brought *into my sanctuary* strangers, uncircumcised in heart, and uncircumcised in flesh, to be in my sanctuary, to pollute it, *even* my house, when ye offer my bread, the fat and the blood, and they have broken my covenant because of all your abominations.

⁸And ye have not kept the charge of mine holy things: but ye have set keepers of my charge in my sanctuary for yourselves.

⁹Thus saith the Lord GOD; No stranger, uncircumcised in heart, nor uncircumcised in flesh, shall enter into my sanctuary, of any stranger that is among the children of Israel.

¹⁰And the Levites that are gone away far from me, when Israel went astray, which went astray away from me after their idols; they shall even bear their iniquity.

¹¹Yet they shall be ministers in my

sanctuary, *having* charge at the gates of the house, and ministering to the house: they shall slay the burnt offering and the sacrifice for the people, and they shall stand before them to minister unto them.

¹²Because they ministered unto them before their idols, and caused the house of Israel to fall into iniquity; therefore have I lifted up mine hand against them, saith the Lord GOD, and they shall bear their iniquity.

¹³And they shall not come near unto me, to do the office of a priest unto me, nor to come near to any of my holy things, in the most holy *place*: but they shall bear their shame, and their abominations which they have committed.

¹⁴But I will make them keepers of the charge of the house, for all the service thereof, and for all that shall be done therein.

¹⁵But the priests the Levites, the sons of Zadok, that kept the charge of my sanctuary when the children of Israel went astray from me, they shall come near to me to minister unto me, and they shall stand before me to offer unto me the fat and the blood, saith the Lord GOD:

¹⁶They shall enter into my sanctuary, and they shall come near to my table, to minister unto me, and they shall keep my charge.

¹⁷And it shall come to pass, *that* when they enter in at the gates of the inner court, they shall be clothed with linen garments; and no

The Sons of Zadok

wool shall come upon them, whiles they minister in the gates of the inner court, and within.

^{18}They shall have linen bonnets upon their heads, and shall have linen breeches upon their loins; they shall not gird *themselves* with any thing that causeth sweat.

^{19}And when they go forth into the utter court, *even* into the utter court to the people, they shall put off their garments wherein they ministered, and lay them in the holy chambers, and they shall put on other garments; and they shall not sanctify the people with their garments.

^{20}Neither shall they shave their heads, nor suffer their locks to grow long; they shall only poll their heads.

^{21}Neither shall any priest drink wine, when they enter into the inner court.

22Neither shall they take for their wives a widow, nor her that is put away: but they shall take maidens of the seed of the house of Israel, or a widow that had a priest before.

^{23}And they shall teach my people *the difference* between the holy and profane, and cause them to discern between the unclean and the clean.

^{24}And in controversy they shall stand in judgment; *and* they shall judge it according to my judgments: and they shall keep my laws and my statutes in all mine assemblies; and they shall hallow my sabbaths.

^{25}And they shall come at no dead person to defile themselves: but for father, or for mother, or for son, or for daughter, for brother, or for sister that hath had no husband, they may defile themselves. (Ezek. 44:1-25)

It all started one late evening in my trailer, for that is what I live in and travel in as an evangelist. It had been a long day and just as I was getting ready to go to bed I stopped and realized that I had not read my Bible for that day.

With a big sigh, the thought crossed my mind to just skip it for that day. My flesh really liked that idea. But, by the grace of God, I decided to go ahead and read my ten pages for that day. Then I realized that I was in the last chapters of Ezekiel. Another groan and sigh was registered in my spirit.

"Well," I thought, *"it is all the word of God and maybe God will give me something from it."* So I started reading about the Temple, knowing that what I was reading was the description of the Jewish Temple that will be built at the beginning of the Millennium.

Now, some parts of the Bible are more interesting to read than other parts. David and Goliath, Gideon and his mighty men, the Red Sea crossing, as well as the Gospels and much of the New Testament, I find all very interesting to read. But you must admit, portions of the Bible such as the genealogies in Chronicles, and other places, such as the last ten chapters of Ezekiel, can be tedious reading at times.

So I dutifully started my Bible reading for that day. By the time I reached Ezekiel 44, I was beginning to

The Sons of Zadok

nod. You know, the head bounce as you fall asleep, then wake up and go on with your reading. I was at this point and then read,

> ^{15}But the priests the Levites, the sons of Zadok, that kept the charge of my sanctuary when the children of Israel went astray from me, they shall come near to me to minister unto me, and they shall stand before me to offer unto me the fat and the blood, saith the Lord GOD:
>
> ^{16}They shall enter into my sanctuary, and they shall come near to my table, to minister unto me, and they shall keep my charge. (Ezek. 44:15-16)

I then stopped reading and thought to myself, *"Wait, what was that? The sons of Zadok? They must be pretty special people if they are the only ones the Lord wants around him in the Millenium."*

I then began to study the sons of Zadok. No, not all that night, but I did make some notes for later, which I used and began what is the basis for this book. It all started one very sleepy evening, and has become a very great blessing to me.

We have now reached the heart of this book. As we begin, remember that the sons of Zadok are Jews. They are not Christians, so we must rightly divide the word of God in this regard, yet we must also not over divide and thus "throw out" the gems of truth found within these scriptures. There will be doctrinal truths for these Jews that will not doctrinally apply to Christians. That being true and accepting they are a very important part of the millennial kingdom, yet there are some great

The Sons of Zadok

truths about them that will spiritually apply to you and me. These truths are very sobering and will directly apply to Christians right now in this Laodicean time in which we live.

Now let me explain what caught my interest as I read that night. In Ezekiel 44:15 notice the following: "**...that kept the charge of my sanctuary when the children of Israel went astray from me....**" They kept the charge of God's sanctuary when the children of Israel went astray. In other words, the sons of Zadok remained faithful during this time. They were the only ones who did. And because they were faithful, it is the sons of Zadok that are the only ones who the Lord Jesus Christ will allow to come into His sanctuary, and minister unto Him during the 1000 years. Wow! Now, you must admit that is an amazing position and designation to have placed upon you by the Lord Jesus Christ!

As the Millennium begins, there are portions of land that are assigned to the twelve tribes of Israel. The Land divisions basically are straight lines that go from **the Mediterranean Sea, straight across to the Euphrates River.** Each tribe is given this land. But in the midst of this land, around Jerusalem, is a special piece of real estate where Jesus Christ will rule and reign over the earth for 1000 years.

[I am not going to spend a lot of time on the divisions of the land and so on. That would detract from the main reason for this book.]

In this portion of real estate will be the Temple of the Lord, and thus the sanctuary of the Lord where Jesus will abide. In this Temple will be the sons of Zadok. *They will minister to Jesus Christ, and be gathered around*

99

The Sons of Zadok

his table. Of His priests, **they are the only ones He will allow around him during this 1000-year reign.** You must admit, that is an amazing reward for 30 years of faithful service.

A priest could only serve in the priesthood from the age of 20 years to 50 years old. So a 30-year service will result in a 1000-year blessing. Do you get the message? You may get saved and live for Jesus Christ for 80 years, but they will have an effect on what you do for 1000 years during the Millenium. This is what I meant about the great truths that will apply to you and me as we study about the sons of Zadok.

It all begins with Zadok, who was a priest during the reign of King David. He is the patriarch of this line of faithful priests in Israel.

The composer, George Frederic Handel, wrote an anthem titled "Zadok the Priest." He composed it for the coronation of King George II in 1727. "Zadok the Priest" has been sung prior to the anointing of the sovereign at the coronation of every British monarch since its composition. It has become recognized as a British patriotic anthem.

> [24] And lo Zadok also, and all the Levites *were* with him, bearing the ark of the covenant of God: and they set down the ark of God; and Abiathar went up, until all the people had done passing out of the city.
>
> [25] And the king said unto Zadok, Carry back the ark of God into the city: if I shall find favour in the eyes of the LORD, he will bring me again, and shew me *both* it, and his habitation:

The Sons of Zadok

The Millennial Inheritance for the Nation of Israel
1000 years in the Land
1000 years of world peace
Ezek. 48:1-35
...the name of the city from that day shall be, The LORD is there.

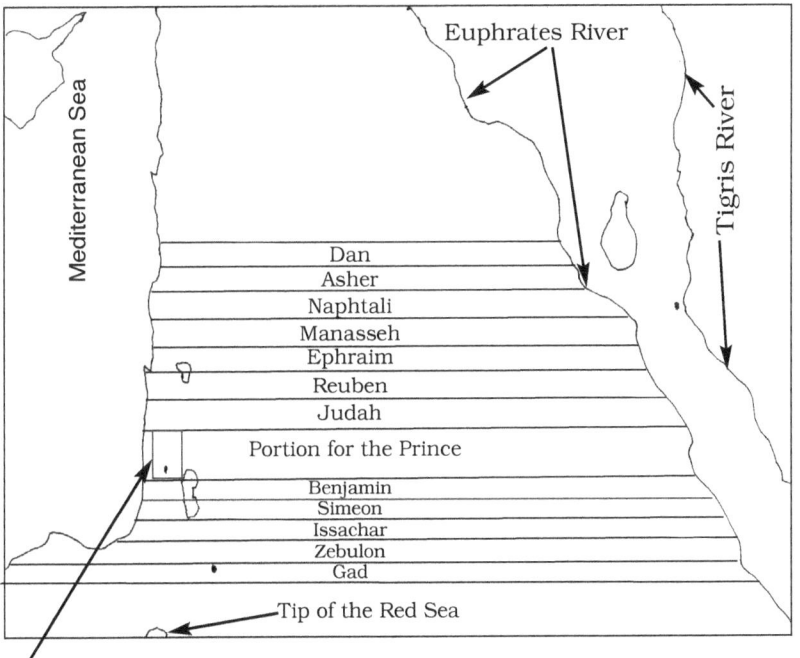

Sanctuary of the Lord - Jerusalem

This is where the Temple of the Lord will be, and this is where the sons of Zadok will minister to the Lord and sit at His table.

The Sons of Zadok

>²⁶But if he thus say, I have no delight in thee; behold, *here am* I, let him do to me as seemeth good unto him.
>
>²⁷The king said also unto Zadok the priest, *Art not* thou a seer? return into the city in peace, and your two sons with you, Ahimaaz thy son, and Jonathan the son of Abiathar.
>(2 Sam. 15:24-27)

What follows may seem a bit tedious, but I want to be thorough in this study and show how that the sons of Zadok were always faithful to the Lord. Zadok is the son of Ahitub and his name is first mentioned in 2 Sam. 8:17. But here in 2 Sam. 15 is the first recorded event and gives us a window into the character of Zadok.

David had committed adultery with Bathsheba and now he is reaping from that sin. His son Absalom has created an insurrection in the kingdom. David has decided to leave in spite of his mighty men being ready to fight.

>¹⁵And the king's servants said unto the king, Behold, **thy servants *are ready to do* whatsoever my lord the king shall appoint.**
>(2 Sam. 15:15)

In other words, *"Your Majesty, we are not afraid and are ready to fight, but we will obey whatever you command."* But David decides to leave. As he is leaving and by this time he has passed over the brook Kidron, here comes Zadok and all the Levites carrying the Ark of God.

This is special, for the Ark of God had the presence of God on it. It was to be carried by the priests only, which is how they were carrying it. David and his

The Sons of Zadok

priests were reminded of that when they went down to Kirjath-jearim to bring up the Ark. Instead of carrying it up according to God's instructions, they put it on a new cart that was being pulled by oxen. A man ended up dead that day.

So here they bring the Ark, set it down, and Zadok comes to King David. But King David tells him to take the Ark back to its place in the Temple. David is surrendered to whatever the Lord has for him. But the thing to notice here is that Zadok is right there with the Ark of God. He is faithful and he knows who the rightful king is. Obediently he carries the Ark back.

Well, some years have gone by, and King David is now up in years. Another one of his sons has the big idea that he is going to be king. His name is Adonijah. And as he attempts to take over the kingdom, he is able to get some of David's officers to follow him, Joab the kings general being one of them. But Zadok does not go with Adonijah. He stays with King David, for Zadok is a faithful man.

David the king establishes Solomon as the rightful king, and thus Soloman takes the throne. His main priest is Azariah who is a son of Zadok.

After many years go by, Israel falls into apostasy. Then a man sits on the throne by the name of Hezekiah, and he is one of the best kings. It is an amazing thing to observe since Hezekiah's father, Ahaz, was one of the worst kings Judah ever had.

Ahaz dies, and the day finally arrives for Hezekiah to be coronated as the new king. This was always a big deal, and rightfully so. But I picture the ceremony taking place with Hezekiah impatient and commanding

The Sons of Zadok

the people to hurry up.

The looks on their faces were looks of perplexity, for they did not understand why the king was so impatient. It was as if he did not even care about the ceremony, nor the accolades of praise that were traditionally given to the new king. As the ceremony was coming to the end, the king speaks up and asks, *"Are you done?"*

"Yes, your majesty, we are done" came back the reply. *"You are now officially the king of Judah."*

Without hesitation, the king commanded the priests to come forth. It was the very first command king Hezekiah gave.

His first command was to have the priests cleanse themselves, and then get the Temple cleansed and back in service for the Lord.

> [3]He [Hezekiah] in **the first year of his reign, in the first month,** opened the doors of the house of the LORD, and repaired them. (2 Chr. 29:3)
>
> [5]And said unto them, **Hear me, ye Levites, sanctify now yourselves, and sanctify the house of the LORD God of your fathers, and carry forth the filthiness out of the holy place.** (2 Chr. 29:5)
>
> [17]Now **they began on the first day of the first month** to sanctify, and on the eighth day of the month came they to the porch of the LORD: so they sanctified the house of the LORD in eight days; and in the sixteenth day of the first month they made an end. (2 Chr. 29:17)
>
> [12]Then the Levites arose, Mahath the son of

The Sons of Zadok

Amasai, and Joel the son of Azariah... (2 Chr. 29:12)

Hezekiah's charge to the priests -

> ^{11}**My sons, be not now negligent: for the LORD hath chosen you to stand before him, to serve him, and that ye should minister unto him, and burn incense.** (2 Chr. 29:11)

This is a great verse! As a Christian, you are a son of God. You are also a priest, for you have direct access to God. Your body is the temple of the Holy Ghost.

> ^{19}What? know ye not that your body is **the temple of the Holy Ghost *which is* in you**, which ye have of God, and ye are not your own? (1 Cor. 6:19)

We live in an age where the temple of the Lord is being neglected. No, I am not talking about pumping iron, working out, and making sure that this *"worm food"* is in tiptop shape. But the temple of the Lord today is being neglected by not exercising it unto godliness.

Part of the Jewish priestly service was to keep the lights burning on the candlestick. There were no windows into the holy place in the Temple of the Lord. When the candlestick went out, it was very dark in there. That candlestick is a type of the Holy Spirit. The word of God states,

> ^{16}Let your light so shine before men, that they may see your good works, and glorify your Father which is in heaven. (Matt. 5:16)

In order for the candles to continue burning you must trim them according to Matthew. What does that mean? Repenting and getting sin out of your life. Without a continual examination of yourself and repenting of sin

The Sons of Zadok

your light will go out. The Holy Spirit will be quenched in your life and body. Today many Christians are spiritually dark because they are not judging themselves, repenting, and confessing their sins to Jesus Christ.

Hezekiah also admonished the priests that not only were they chosen to stand before the Lord, but they were also to serve Him as well. Do you see how applicable these truths are for us today? No, we do not have a physical temple of brick and mortar, but our bodies are the temple of the Lord, and we are to use these bodies to serve the Lord.

> [1]Now there were **in the church** that was at Antioch certain prophets and teachers; as Barnabas, and Simeon that was called Niger, and Lucius of Cyrene, and Manaen, which had been brought up with Herod the tetrarch, and Saul.
>
> [2]**As they ministered to the Lord**, and fasted, the Holy Ghost said, Separate me Barnabas and Saul for the work whereunto I have called them. (Acts 13:1-2)

When you work in your local church, you are ministering to the Lord. Much of the Labor of a church is ministering the word of God to people. When you have a part in that, you are not only ministering to people, but you are ministering to the Lord. The majority of the time, when a Christian is not in a local church, they are not serving the Lord.

You may be in a place where there is no Bible Believing church to attend. What should you do? The first thing is to remember this: the right church is the

The Sons of Zadok

one God wants you in. You must surrender to God's will, go by your King James Bible, and minister in the church God wants you attending.

The second thing to remember is that if there is no church to attend in your area, then start one. Or at least start a Bible study and pray for the Lord to send a pastor.

Thirdly, if you are not going to start a church then you need to move to where there is a church for you and your family to attend. It is more important than your house and monthly income. Amen!

And these priests were to burn incense. Incense in the word of God is a picture of prayer.

> ^{10}And the whole multitude of the people were **praying without at the time of incense.** (Luke 1:10)
>
> ^{8}...golden vials full of **odours, which are the prayers** of saints. (Rev. 5:8)
>
> ^{3}And another angel came and stood at the altar, having a golden censer; and there was given unto him much **incense**, that he should offer *it* with the **prayers of all saints** upon the golden altar which was before the throne.
>
> ^{4}And the smoke of the **incense**, *which came* with **the prayers of the saints**, ascended up before God out of the angel's hand. (Rev. 8:3-4)

In these last days before the calling out of the body of Christ, there is very little real praying going on. Dear reader, when is the last time you got alone with the Lord and spent one hour in prayer, praying out loud to him? How much time do you spend each day alone in prayer with your Saviour?

Are you too busy? No, it is called neglect. Your

The Sons of Zadok

temple is being neglected, and in such cases the lights go out. The problem is that most of God's people are so far removed from a close walk with their Lord that they are not even aware that they are not in fellowship with him.

I have been around church buildings that had been closed down, or close to it. A new church bought the building and went in to clean it up and there were devils and marks of devils in the church.

In one church, there were strange sounds to the point that they called the police to investigate it. Another church had a mascot painted on the wall of a black panther with blood dripping out of its' mouth. After the new church started meeting, and the building was occupied often with praying Christians, eventually the devils left and a good Spirit was restored to the building.

As these priests go into the Temple, they begin to clean it. The filth and defilement in the Temple was horrible, but they labored and labored from early in the morning to late at night. For eight days they worked. And as they worked, do you know what happened? They got very dirty and sweaty! Let me say that again. They got very dirty and sweaty.

You may ask, *"Why did you repeat that, and why did you write that?"* Well, we'll get to that a little later, but don't forget that! You see, we are studying what a Christian will do in the Millenium. This story has a very great application, but I must conceal it for now.

So they work and work, and guess who is among the priests working in the Temple. It was a man by the name of Joel, the son of Azariah. Joel the son of

The Sons of Zadok

Azariah was a son of Zadok. (2 Chron. 31:10, 29:12) Perhaps you notice that there were many other priests who were also present and working, sweating and getting dirty, and that is true. But as time goes by, the number dwindles down to only the sons of Zadok remaining faithful in the service of the Lord.

Well, more years go by, and Israel falls back into apostasy again. Another new king comes on the scene by the name of Josiah. Josiah is eight years old when he begins to reign. Can you imagine being eight years old and being in charge of a nation? In this age, an eight year old would probably have more sense than the political leaders of our day. At least he wouldn't be ruined by a college education. (Not everybody that goes to college is ruined, just most of them.)

> ¹Josiah *was* eight years old when he began to reign, and he reigned thirty and one years in Jerusalem. And his mother's name *was* Jedidah, the daughter of Adaiah of Boscath.
>
> ²And **he did *that which was* right in the sight of the LORD**, and walked in all the way of David his father, and turned not aside to the right hand or to the left.
>
> ³And it came to pass in the eighteenth year of king Josiah, *that* the king sent Shaphan the son of Azaliah, the son of Meshullam, the scribe, to the house of the LORD, saying,
>
> ⁴Go up to **Hilkiah the high priest,** that he may sum the silver which is brought into the house of the LORD, which the keepers of the

The Sons of Zadok

door have gathered of the people:

⁵And let them deliver it into the hand of the doers of the work, that have the oversight of the house of the LORD: and let them give it to the doers of the work which *is* in the house of the LORD, to repair the breaches of the house,

⁶Unto carpenters, and builders, and masons, and to buy timber and hewn stone to repair the house.

⁷Howbeit there was no reckoning made with them of the money that was delivered into their hand, because they dealt faithfully.

⁸And **Hilkiah the high priest said unto Shaphan the scribe, I have found the book of the law in the house of the LORD. And Hilkiah gave the book to Shaphan**, and he read it.

⁹And Shaphan the scribe came to the king, and brought the king word again, and said, Thy servants have gathered the money that was found in the house, and have delivered it into the hand of them that do the work, that have the oversight of the house of the LORD. (2 Kings 22:1-9)

Josiah gives the order that the Temple of God is to be repaired. The high priest at this time is a man by the name of Hilkiah. This priest is by himself now. The other priests are gone and guess what, Hilkiah is a son of Zadok. (1 Chron. 6:12-13)

By this time in the life of the nation of Israel, you are reading about a period that is just a few years before

The Sons of Zadok

they get taken away to Babylon. You are reading about the end of Israel dwelling in the promised land.

Israel does return to the land under the leadership of Nehemiah, but they are never under their own control. There is always another nation ruling over them...until 1948. Israel came back into their land in 1948 with no other nation ruling over them.

The time here though, under the reign of Josiah, is very similar to the days in which we live today as Christians. We are in the last moments before the Lord calls us out of the world. Christianity is in apostasy. The vast majority of Christianity does not even know where the word of God is. They do not believe, for the most part that we even have the inerrant word of God. It is the word of God that is the foundation for everything that we believe. Without the word of God we are helpless, hopeless and weak, for we are disarmed. No weapon!

By the grace of God I am not disarmed, for I know where the inerrant word of God is; I have a copy of it that I read every day. It is the Authorized Version of 1611. That is the inerrant word of God, but the vast majority do not believe they even have the word of God. Because of this, the church today is powerless, and filthy.

So when you read about Josiah, you are reading about the last years before the taking away to Babylon. At this time there is a priest there by the name of Hilkiah, and he is a son of Zadok. Again, the temple is being repaired and cleaned, and guess what. They got dirty! And they got sweaty! You may ask, *"Why do you write that?"* Well, there is a good reason, but I can't let

The Sons of Zadok

you know right now, but you will in a little further on in this book.

As they are cleaning the temple, Hilkiah-this son of Zadok-proclaims to Shaphan, *"I have found the book of the law in the house of the Lord."* This is a great find. It is always a great find when you realize where the word of God is. The word of God is the most valuable, physical thing on the face of this earth!!! I am not kidding. Stop and think about what the word of God is. Weigh in your mind how you are to appear before God one day at the Judgement. It is this word of God that will instruct and guide you in this life so that you will make it through the judgement in a proper manner.

You see, Hilkiah is not only a son of Zadok when all the other priests are gone, but he is also a Bible believer. He knows where the word of God is, and he is excited about it. He gives it to Shaphan and tells him to take it to the king. From this a revival breaks out.

Hilkiah is used greatly by the Lord and also fathers a son who is used greatly, and that son is Jeremiah. Yes, Jeremiah is a son of Zadok, and he preaches during the time of Josiah, as well as the kings that come after Josiah. Jeremiah is there when Israel gets taken to Babylon.

> [1]The words of **Jeremiah the son of Hilkiah**, of the **priests** that *were* in Anathoth in the land of Benjamin:
>
> [2]To whom the word of the LORD came in **the days of Josiah** the son of Amon king of Judah, in the thirteenth year of his reign.
>
> [3]It came also in the days of Jehoiakim the

The Sons of Zadok

son of Josiah king of Judah, unto the end of the eleventh year of Zedekiah the son of Josiah king of Judah, unto the carrying away of Jerusalem captive in the fifth month. (Jer. 1:1-3)

Jeremiah, also referred to by some as the weeping prophet, is faithful to the Lord during his ministry. It was not easy for Jeremiah to be faithful, especially when the other priests were actually working against him.

⁷**So the priests and the prophets and all the people heard Jeremiah speaking these words in the house of the LORD.**

⁸Now it came to pass, when Jeremiah had made an end of speaking all that the LORD had commanded *him* to speak unto all the people, that the priests and the prophets and all the people took him, saying, **Thou shalt surely die.** (Jer. 26:7-8)

⁶Then took they Jeremiah, and cast him into the dungeon of Malchiah the son of Hammelech, that *was* in the court of the prison: and they let down Jeremiah with cords. And in the dungeon *there was* no water, but mire: so **Jeremiah sunk in the mire.** (Jer. 38:6)

Jeremiah is constantly attacked, persecuted, and even tortured while obeying the Lord in warning Israel of what was coming, and what they should do. Over and over he would preach, and standing in front of him amongst the crowds of people, would be *fellow priests.* Priests standing *with the people* and not standing with

113

The Sons of Zadok

Jeremiah, thus not standing with the Lord. They were more concerned about pleasing the people and having a house, than they were concerned about obeying and being faithful to the Lord. Because of this, you will see what the Lord does to them during the Millennium.

Jeremiah also prophesied for Israel to submit to the king of Babylon, Nebuchadnezzar.

> [12] I spake also to Zedekiah king of Judah according to all these words, saying, **Bring your necks under the yoke of the king of Babylon, and serve him and his people, and live.** (Jer. 27:12)

Now when Jeremiah prophesied that they should submit to the king of Babylon, there were other sons of Zadok who heard him prophecy this from the mouth of the Lord. When they heard this they asked, Jeremiah, *"Hey bro, is that really what the Lord is commanding us to do?"* To which Jeremiah responded, *"Thus saith the Lord! Yes, it is. And not only that, but you are to marry wives, get houses and plant crops while you are there."*

They then got their few possessions together and said, *"Well, OK, if that is what the Lord wants, then we will obey Him."* And off to Babylon they went. After some years of living in Babylon, Israel gets the message that God does not tolerate idolatry. They realize idolatry is the reason why God sent them to captivity in Babylon.

The three Hebrew children-Shadrach, Meshach, and Abednego-are faced with death in the fiery furnace if they do not bow down to the idol that King Nebuchadnezzar has built. At the sound of the music they were to fall down and worship the golden image. But if not, then they would be cast into the burning

The Sons of Zadok

fiery furnace. Notice the answer they give when the choice of idolatry or death is set before them.

¹⁶Shadrach, Meshach, and Abed-nego, answered and said to the king, O Nebuchadnezzar, **we *are* not careful to answer thee in this matter.**

¹⁷If it be so, our God whom we serve is able to deliver us from the burning fiery furnace, and he will deliver *us* out of thine hand, O king.

¹⁸But if not, be it known unto thee, O king, that **we will not serve thy gods, nor worship the golden image which thou hast set up.** (Dan. 3:16-18)

They were resolved in their hearts that they were not going to worship the image. They did not have to debate the matter for they knew exactly what they were going to do. They said, *"No!"*

The Bible states that God is a jealous God. It states in Exod. 34:14, **"...the Lord, whose name is Jealous."** That's right, one of God's names is Jealous. When a person commits idolatry, either by making graven images, or by being covetous, then according to the word of God, that person hates God. And idolatry is a major reason many Christians will lose their reward in the Millennium. What I write here is very serious and will have an effect on whether you reign with Jesus Christ for 1000 years on this earth, or whether you don't.

The second commandment is to not make unto thee any graven image, and you are not to bow down unto them. Your Jealous God will be very upset. Below is the

The Sons of Zadok

second commandment:

> ⁴Thou shalt not make unto thee any graven image, or any likeness *of anything* that *is* in heaven above, or that is in the earth beneath, or that *is* in the water under the earth:
>
> ⁵Thou shalt not bow down thyself to them, **nor serve them**: for I the LORD thy God *am* a jealous God, visiting the iniquity of the fathers upon the children unto the third and fourth *generation* of **them that hate me;**
>
> ⁶And shewing mercy unto thousands of them that love me, and keep my commandments. (Ex. 20:4-6)

Make sure you notice the words I highlighted, "**...of them that hate me...**" Someone who uses graven images to worship God, or falls down to them actually hates God. It is interesting to note the Roman Catholic Church removed the second commandment.

Here are the Catholic Ten Commandments:

1   I am the LORD your God. You shall worship the Lord your God and Him only shall you serve.

2   You shall not take the name of the Lord your God in vain.

3   Remember to keep holy the Sabbath day.

4   Honor your father and your mother.

5   You shall not kill.

6   You shall not commit adultery.

7   You shall not steal.

8   You shall not bear false witness against your neighbor.

The Sons of Zadok

    9   You shall not covet your neighbor's wife.
    10   You shall not covet your neighbor's goods.
(http://www.beginningcatholic.com/catholic-ten-commandments)

This is the traditional version of the commandments according to the Catholic Church. It is the version ascribed to by St. Augustine. You will notice the second commandment has been moved up to the third commandment's place. The tenth commandment has been split into two, thus making it the ninth and tenth commandments. Somebody does not want it to be known that God says they actually hate God. Of course, if you asked them they would proclaim loudly that they love God, but their works proclaim, according to the word of God, that they hate God. So why am I going into all of this? I will show you why.

To worship graven images is idolatry and God hates it. But idolatry, as defined in the word of God does not stop with graven idols. Keep in mind, that those who worship idols proclaim by their works that they hate God. There is an idolatry rampant in the world today and it is the major mark of the Laodicean time in which we live. Notice what the word of God says:

> ^{5}Mortify therefore your members which are upon the earth; fornication, uncleanness, inordinate affection, evil concupiscence, and **covetousness, which is idolatry:** (Col. 3:5)
>
> ^{24}No man can serve two masters: for either **he will hate the one, and love the other;** or else he will **hold to the one, and despise the other.** Ye cannot serve God and mammon. (Matt. 6:24)

If you will let those two verses sink down into your

soul, you will find them very sobering. There are many Christians today who would proclaim loudly that they love their Lord Jesus Christ, but they proclaim that as long as they have money in the bank and live in a nice house. But when the funds are low, and they have to live out of a car, it becomes a different matter.

There are many men today who have been called by God to preach, but they won't surrender their life to the Lord. The problem is they don't want to do without. They have been given the highest calling on earth, which is the call to preach and they don't want to give anything up in order to fulfill God's call on their life. Their works proclaim that they hate God.

These verses though, are not limited to men called to preach. These verses are written to all Christians. If you are saved, then you are to put Jesus Christ first; if you do that you may have to give up some earthly comforts. It's not always big things you have to give up, but it will be things that YOU KNOW ARE WRONG. It could be a church God wants you to join, or a job He wants you to quit because it is not right. But you will know what it is that Jesus Christ wants you to do. You cannot serve God and mammon. It is impossible. When you choose to go against God, and His will for your life, then you are committing idolatry. Especially if the reason you disobey your Saviour has to do with money and things.

The Roman Catholics are idolaters because they use statues, and bow down to statues. They kiss statues of Mary and so on, and we call them idolaters for doing so. But born again Christians are just as big of idolaters as the Roman Catholics, for Christians are bowing down

The Sons of Zadok

to money and things. With excuses like, *"I have to work, so I can't make it to church."* Idolatry! *"We can't get married because if we do then we will lose money and our monthly income will drop."* Idolater! *"If I surrender to the Lord's will, I will lose my house."* Idolater! And really what you are saying, by your works, is that you hate the very God that saved your wicked soul from Hell.

Jeremiah-a son of Zadok-does right, even when the other priests are not doing right. Jeremiah is persecuted severely, but he does right.

After years of living in captivity, the Lord leads a remnant of Israel back to the promised land under the leadership of Nehemiah. But along with Nehemiah is a priest by the name of Ezra, and guess what? Ezra is a son of Zadok. The sons of Zadok always did right and served the Lord. At times, the other priests of Israel who were not doing right, would gang up on the priests, the sons of Zadok, that were doing right.

This brings us to an amazing portion of scripture found in Ezekiel 44. The sons of Zadok are mentioned here, but so are the other priests, the unfaithful priests. This scripture will take place at the beginning of the Millennium. The Tribulation is over, Jesus Christ has come back to this earth and destroyed the armies of the Anti-Christ. It is now judgement time. As with these priests, remember, one day you will give an account of what you did for the Lord. And one day, you will be given rewards, or you will hang your head in shame when you lose your rewards. Your works will tell exactly whether you loved the Lord or not.

In Ezekiel 44:1-3 you have the prophecy of the Lord Jesus Christ entering through the eastern gate. He will

The Sons of Zadok

do this at the start of the Millennium when He sets foot upon this earth. If the Lord came today and called His born again people out of this world, then what you are reading would only be seven years away.

So now notice the following verse:

> [10]**And the Levites** that are gone away far from me, **when Israel went astray,** which went astray away from me after their idols; they shall even bear their iniquity. (Ezek. 44:10)

"**And the Levites...**" The Levites had the charge of the care of the sanctuary of the Lord, but they were also the priests. And not all of the Levites will make it into the Millennium. Some ended up in Hell, such as Dathan, Abiram, and Korah. They rebelled against Moses and Aaron, and the earth opened its mouth and swallowed them alive down into the pit of Hell. (See Num. 16) This is one example to show that not all of the priests will make it into the Millennium. Exactly what the line was that was crossed that would cause them to end up in Hell, I don't know. I know with these three it was rebellion against God's leadership through Moses and Aaron.

Another thing to notice about this story is that Dathan and Abiram had their entire family with each of them, and their entire family descended into Hell. But Korah's children did not descend into Hell, for in the book of Psalms you have Psalms written to the sons of Korah. So Korah's kids did not side with daddy, they sided with Moses and the Lord.

God has given each of us a free will, and it is your choice whether you will obey the Lord or someone else.

The Sons of Zadok

Many times family will cause people to go against the Lord, with many of them ending up in Hell because of it.

In Ezekiel 44 we are dealing with Jews, but there are many lessons that will be learned here that will apply to Christians.

I was preaching my sermon on the sons of Zadok, and specifically this portion of scripture. As I preached verse by verse through the chapter, I failed to clearly make the case that we are dealing with Jews here, not Christians doctrinally. So when the Lord proclaims 44:13 "**...and they shall not come near unto** ," I failed to make that distinction clearly. The pastor had a dear sister in the Lord call him that night in tears, afraid that Jesus was going to push her away and not let her be near him for 1000 years. Yes, I can understand how that would put you into tears, but that is not going to happen to a Christian. It will happen to some Jewish priests, but not to a Christian.

There is a group of "Baptists" that believe the unfaithful Christians will be in outer darkness weeping and wailing and gnashing their teeth for 1000 years. Let me clearly proclaim, that is also a complete lie! (1 Thess. 4:16)

So in verse 10 you have Levites that are gone far away from the Lord. They went away with Israel after their idols. The Lord tells them that they are going to bear their iniquity. How long will they bear their iniquity? Oh! One Thousand years! They made it into the Millennium and that is good. But in the Millennium, it is going to be obvious to all that they did not love the Lord enough to be faithful to Him for 30 years.

What follows is very important!

The Sons of Zadok

A Christian may get saved as a young boy or girl, or they may get saved late in life, but how they live for Jesus Christ will have a direct effect on how they live during the Millennium. It will be obvious whether you loved your Saviour or not. It will be obvious whether you obeyed His call on your life or not.

Dear brother or sister in the Lord, you need to stop and think about that! Are you in God's perfect will for your life, and are you doing what He has called you to do?

> ¹⁴These shall make war with the Lamb, and the Lamb shall overcome them: for he is Lord of lords, and King of kings: and they that are with him *are* **called, and chosen, and faithful.** (Rev. 17:14)

Yes, you are called by Jesus Christ. Have you answered that call? If you have not, it will be made manifest for 1000 years. You need to think about that!

The emphasis in the world today is to live for today. Capture the moment. If it feels good, do it, and so on. Well, for a Christian you will regret it one day if that is how you are living your Christian life.

Now, notice verse 11.

> ¹¹Yet they shall be ministers in my sanctuary, *having* charge at the gates of the house, and **ministering to the house: they shall slay the burnt offering** and the sacrifice for the people, and they shall stand before them to minister unto them.
>
> ¹²**Because** they ministered unto them before their idols, and caused the house of Israel to

The Sons of Zadok

fall into iniquity; therefore have **I lifted up mine hand against them**, saith the Lord GOD, and they shall bear their iniquity. (Ezek. 44:11-12)

These Levites-not Christians-minister to the house, slay the burnt offering, sacrifice for the people, and minister to the people. They will do this for 1000 years. Notice the word *"Because"* at the beginning of verse 12. This is why the Lord puts them where He does.

Do you realize, they get what they wanted? They wanted to please *"the people"* when they ministered in the Old Testament, instead of wanting to please the Lord and obey Him in the work He wanted them to do. They even are blamed for leading the nation of Israel astray.

There is a story in Judges 17 about a Levite who enters into the house of Micah. This Levite is sojourning. In other words, he has left the sanctuary of the Lord and is looking for a place to live among the people. He ends up becoming **"...a father and a priest."**

> ^{10}And Micah said unto him, Dwell with me, and be unto me **a father and a priest**, and I will give thee **ten shekels of silver** by the year, and **a suit of apparel**, and **thy victuals**. So the Levite went in. (Judg. 17:10)

He sold out for money, food and clothes. Does he make it into the Millennium? I have no idea. All I know is that he ends up the head of the religion for the tribe of Dan.

> ^{30}And the children of Dan set up the graven image: and Jonathan, the son of Gershom, the son of Manasseh, **he and his sons were priests to the tribe of Dan until the day of**

The Sons of Zadok

the captivity of the land. (Judg. 18:30)

He ministers to the people, for the people, as he seeks to please the people.

So now, it is the Millennium, and the Lord is setting up His kingdom which will last for 1000 years. Before Him are the priests and Levites who have their part in the first resurrection, upon such the second death hath no power. Here they stand as He tells them what they are going to be doing for 1000 years, and do you know what they get? They get what they wanted. That's right, they get what they wanted, at least what they wanted when they lived on this earth in their mortal bodies. What they wanted was to please the people.

They weren't interested in pleasing their God. They weren't interested in serving their God. They merely wanted to please the people: maybe for income, clothes and food? So now they serve the people. That's right, they work for 1000 years serving the people and ministering to the house.

I don't want to get ahead of myself here, but I must bring up a question. If what you get in the Millennium is based upon what you wanted in this life, what will it be? What will you get? When the Lord is giving out cities to Christians to rule and reign over, what will He be giving you? Are you spending your life just to get a house? What if you get what you want, and instead of getting 5 or 10 cities to reign over, you get a house?

Perhaps, in a selfish attitude you say, *"I'm not greedy and a house will be fine!"* Oh, but dear Christian, it will be a shame on you, and it will be obvious for 1000 years that you did not love your Saviour who died for you on the Cross. You did not love Him enough to serve Him

The Sons of Zadok

first. **Your heart's desire, your idol is what you receive.** What will you do for 1000 years?

So here are these Levites, and they are going to get what they want. Well, what they wanted when they lived in their mortal bodies along with its free will.

[11]"...they shall slay the burnt offering..." (Eze. 44:11)

Do you remember the priests under Hezekiah who were ordered to go into the house of the Lord and clean it up? And when they went in there, they got very dirty and sweaty. But they labored and sweated for God.

Do you remember the priest, Hilkiah, a son of Zadok, along with Shaphan the scribe, who went into the Temple and cleaned it up under orders from Josiah? By that time it was just two men, as the other priests and Levites were nowhere to be found. And when they went in to clean it up, they got dirty and sweaty. It was hard, dirty work.

Well, now the Lord is setting up His kingdom for 1000 years. Here are a bunch of Levites and priests before Him, and guess what they get to do for 1000 years? Serve the people and slay the burnt offering.

To slay the burnt offering is to rope, or corral the bullock, goat, or lamb, and then cut their neck and drain the blood from them. It is dirty work. You know, even though it is the Millennium and the atmosphere is different than it was before, yet I would imagine they are going to sweat at times as they go out to slay the burnt offering.

Are you getting the message? Are you doing the job your Saviour Jesus Christ wants you to do? I cannot do your job, and you cannot do mine. But Jesus Christ

The Sons of Zadok

has a job He wants you to do. The King of the universe does not need you or me, and He could do the job much better if He did it himself. But, He has chosen you and asked you to do something for Him.

Do you know what it is? I know what He wants me to do, but I have no idea what He wants you to do. Do you know? If you have been saved for more than a year, why don't you know what He wants you to do? You had better find out before it is too late, and you had better get busy doing God's perfect will for your life.

> [13] And **they shall not come near unto me**, to do the office of a priest unto me, nor to come near to any of my holy things, in the most holy *place*: but they shall bear their shame, and their abominations which they have committed. (Ezek. 44:13)

This is the verse that scared the lady, who in tears called her pastor. Remember though, these are Jews in the Millennium. These are not Christians in the Millennium. But you must admit that is quite a verse and statement from the Lord! **"They shall not come near unto me." "They shall bear their shame and their abominations which they have committed."** The Lord is disgusted with them and does not want them around himself.

How long will they bear their shame Lord? Oh, for 1000 years! Dear reader, you must remember that the tears are not wiped away until AFTER the Millennium. That is found in Revelation 21:4 when there is a new heaven and a new earth. The Millennium of Jesus Christ reigning on this earth is 1000 years long. After that is the White Throne Judgement, and then the new heaven and earth.

¹⁴But I will make them keepers of the **charge of the house**, for all the service thereof, and for all that shall be done therein. (Ezek. 44:14)

So here they are for 1000 years tending to the house. These are the carpenters, the janitors, the plumbers, the painters, etc. They got what they wanted. They were concerned about the physical things, so now they get to tend to the physical things of the house of the Lord. If they would have tended to the physical things of God in the Old Testament, then the Lord would have had something far greater for them at this time.

If you get what you want in the Millennium, what will it be? You also need to remember that at that time you will have a new body and a perfect heart. You will have a great desire to serve and to please your Saviour Jesus Christ.

One of the most heartbreaking events to happen to anyone, is to love someone with all your heart and have a desire to serve them or please them, such as in a marriage or family. But oh, what a heartbreak if the one, in disgust, refuses you and says, *"No, I got someone else to do it."* Oh my, how that hurts!

What is even more heartbreaking is at this time you will know that He is right and just in all of His dealings. He is not mad at you, dear Christian, but He will not use you then, if you do not serve and submit to your Lord Jesus Christ now.

Remember that when Esau comes in and finds out that Jacob got the blessing, he begins to cry. He is

The Sons of Zadok

broken and begs his father to bless him. Isaac does give him a blessing, but it is nowhere near what Jacob got. When the blessings and judgements are given out by the Lord Jesus Christ, He is not mad. It is what it is and you will know His judgements are just and right. You will have no one to blame but yourself.

> [15]**But the priests the Levites, the sons of Zadok, that kept the charge of my sanctuary when the children of Israel went astray from me, they shall come near to me to minister unto me, and they shall stand before me to offer unto me the fat and the blood,** saith the Lord GOD: (Ezek. 44:15)

Now comes the other group. These are the faithful priests, the Levites and the sons of Zadok.

When King Jesus sets up His kingdom upon this earth for 1000 years, He divides the land of Israel and gives each tribe a portion of the land. This portion, and the dwelling of Israel, will be from the Mediterranean Sea all the way across to the Euphrates River. That is modern day Iraq.

In the center of this land grant, which is also known as *"the inheritance"* for the children of Israel, is a very special portion of real estate. It is larger than the other portions, and it is where Jesus Christ will rule and reign from for 1000 years. Within the western side of this land grant is Jerusalem. The area where Jerusalem sits is holy and within this holy portion is the Temple, and thus the sanctuary of the Lord.

> [10]...and **the sanctuary of the LORD** shall be in the midst thereof.
>
> [11]*It shall be* for the priests that are

The Sons of Zadok

sanctified of the sons of Zadok; which have kept my charge, which went not astray when the children of Israel went astray, as the Levites went astray.

> ^{12}And *this* oblation of the land that is offered shall be unto them a thing most holy by the border of the Levites. (Ezek. 48:10-12)

This area where Jerusalem sits will have one way streets. Notice how specific the word of God is concerning these things.

> ^{9}But when the people of the land shall come before the LORD in the solemn feasts, he that entereth in by **the way of the north gate** to worship shall **go out by the way of the south gate;** and he that entereth by **the way of the south gate** shall go forth by **the way of the north gate: he shall not return by the way of the gate whereby he came in,** but shall go forth over against it. (Ezek. 46:9)

The reason for the one-way streets is because Jerusalem will be a very crowded place. People from all over the world will travel there to worship the King, the Lord Jesus Christ. And if people do not travel there to worship the King, then there will be no rain upon their land.

> ^{16}And it shall come to pass, *that* every one that is left of all the nations which came against Jerusalem shall even go up from year to year to worship the King, the LORD of hosts, and to keep the feast of tabernacles.
>
> ^{17}And it shall be, *that* **whoso will not come up** of *all* the families of the earth unto

129

The Sons of Zadok

Jerusalem to worship the King, the LORD of hosts, even **upon them shall be no rain.** (Zech. 14:16-17)

But the attitude of most people during this time will be a great desire to go see and worship the King, the Lord Jesus Christ.

^{21}And the inhabitants of one *city* shall go to another, saying, Let us go speedily to pray before the LORD, and to seek the LORD of hosts: **I will go also.** (Zech. 8:21)

Notice the last part of that verse, "**I will go also.**"

That is a picture of people going to each other and saying, *"let's go worship the Lord."* A reply comes back, *"OK, yes, let's go."* Then someone overhears what they are getting ready to do, and they eagerly speak up and say, *"I will go also."*

Not only that, but waters issue out from under the Temple. Wherever the waters flow to, the place is filled with all kinds of fishes.

^{9}And it shall come to pass, *that* every thing that liveth, which moveth, whithersoever the rivers shall come, shall live: and **there shall be a very great multitude of fish, because these waters shall come thither: for they shall be healed;** and every thing shall live whither the river cometh.

^{10}And it shall come to pass, *that* the fishers shall stand upon it from Engedi even unto Eneglaim; they shall be a *place* to spread forth nets; their fish shall be according to their kinds, as the fish of the great sea, **exceeding many.** (Ezek. 47:9-10)

The Sons of Zadok

Here is another glimpse into this time of 1000 years reign of Jesus Christ on this earth. The streets will be full of children playing.

> ³Thus saith the LORD; I am returned unto Zion, and will dwell in the midst of Jerusalem: and Jerusalem shall be called a city of truth; and the mountain of the LORD of hosts the holy mountain.
>
> ⁴Thus saith the LORD of hosts; **There shall yet old men and old women dwell in the streets of Jerusalem,** and every man with his staff in his hand for very age.
>
> ⁵And the streets of the city shall be full of **boys and girls playing in the streets** thereof. (Zech. 8:3-5)

These portions of scriptures are glimpses into the atmosphere around Jerusalem during the reign of Jesus Christ. It is a happy, joyful time of peace and safety. You see, there is a requirement for peace and safety. The requirement is righteousness, and it always precedes the peace and safety.

During the first coming of Jesus Christ, when He was born in the manger, the angels spoke and proclaimed:

> ¹³And suddenly there was with the angel a multitude of the heavenly host praising God, and saying,
>
> ¹⁴**Glory to God in the highest, and on earth peace**, good will toward men. (Luke 2:13-14)

There will be no peace on earth before there is glory to God in the highest on this earth, and that takes place during the Millennium.

OK, so let's get back to the Lord setting up His

The Sons of Zadok

kingdom. As He is giving out the land to the 12 tribes of Israel, right in the center is a very special portion. It is where Jesus Christ will dwell, and more specifically the center of it will be on the western side with the Temple, and the sanctuary of the Lord in the midst of it. The King, the Lord Jesus Christ, will abide right there. The most High God in all of His glory will abide there. So now notice who is allowed to be in there with Him.

The faithful priests, Levites and the sons of Zadok, are the ones who are allowed to minister in there. They offer the fat and the blood. Yes, during the Millennium the sacrifices are instituted and performed. They are performed as a memorial of what Jesus Christ did on the cross of Calvary, when He was the **"Lamb of God which taketh away the sin of the world."** (John 1:29)

> [15] But the priests the Levites, **the sons of Zadok,** that kept the charge of my sanctuary when the children of Israel went astray from me, they shall come near to me to minister unto me, and they shall stand before me to **offer unto me the fat and the blood,** saith the Lord GOD: (Ezek. 44:15)

These, who had been faithful, now have the joy and privilege to offer the fat and the blood to Jesus Christ. But where do they get that from? Ah yes, do you remember what those who had not been faithful are charged with doing? They are going to have to slay the burnt offering.

> [11] Yet they shall be ministers in my sanctuary, *having* charge at the gates of the house, and ministering to the house: **they**

The Sons of Zadok

> **shall slay the burnt offering and the sacrifice** for the people, and they shall stand before them to minister unto them. (Ezek. 44:11)

After slaying the burnt offering, they take the fat and the blood and bring it to those priests who had been faithful.

Here is what God says about the clothing of the faithful. While the others are slaying the animals and getting dirty preparing the offering of the Lord, the faithful and the sons of Zadok are clean, cool, and comfortable.

> ^{17}And it shall come to pass, *that* when they enter in at the gates of the inner court, they shall be clothed with **linen garments;** and no wool shall come upon them, whiles they minister in the gates of the inner court, and within.
>
> ^{18}They shall have **linen bonnets** upon their heads, and shall have **linen breeches** upon their loins; **they shall not gird** *themselves* **with any thing that causeth sweat.** (Ezek. 44:17-18)

Dear reader, here is the message you need to get. In so many words, God says,

"I remember the times when you cleaned up the house of God for me. The times you got sweaty and dirty while you were doing right. I remember the reproach you bore for me when the other priests abandoned my sanctuary. But you stayed faithful and true to me, so now here are special clean clothes for you to wear. Beautiful clothes to wear to keep you cool and clean. And I do not want you to sweat.

The Sons of Zadok

You did that for me when others wouldn't, so now you are to be clean, cool, and comfortable."

Dear Christian, it is time to work now. It is time to bear reproach for Jesus Christ now. It is time to clean the church, clean your heart, and labor in the field for the Master. There is another day coming, and then it will be time to rest, reign and rejoice in your Lord.

Now, here is a very extraordinary thing that the Lord mentions.

> [15] But the priests the Levites, the sons of Zadok, that kept the charge of my sanctuary when the children of Israel went astray from me, they shall come near to me to minister unto me, and **they shall stand before me to offer unto me the fat and the blood**, saith the Lord GOD:
>
> [16] **They shall enter into my sanctuary, and they shall come near to my table, to minister unto me, and they shall keep my charge.** (Ezek. 44:15-16)
>
> [10] ...the sanctuary of the LORD shall be in the midst thereof.
>
> [11] **It shall be for the priests that are sanctified of the sons of Zadok;** which have kept my charge, which went not astray when the children of Israel went astray, as the Levites went astray. (Ezek. 48:10-11)

In the sanctuary of the Lord sits the Lord Jesus Christ at His table. Round table? I doubt it! Probably a long, majestic table with Jesus Christ seated at the head of the table, clothed in beautiful garments down

The Sons of Zadok

to the feet. His face shines bright, and light beams out from under His garments at His feet, His arms and His neck. Wherever the clothing stops, glorious light beams out from under it. The room is bright with light, for there is no darkness there. The Light of the World abides in that sanctuary.

And there is only one group of men that the Lord will allow to minister unto Him in that sanctuary, and those are the sons of Zadok. (Ezek. 48:11)

Is He a respecter of persons? Not now He isn't. But then, during that 1000-year reign, He rewards those who have been faithful. They all had their chance to prove their love for Him, but it was the sons of Zadok who proved true to Him. This is their inheritance. This is their reward, and, my oh my, what a reward it is!

The priests who did not serve Him then, will serve Him now! For 1000 years. The priests who did not serve him for 30 years then, will serve Him for 1000 years at this time. What a reaping!

Christian, are you serving Him now? Maybe you got saved when you were young, but what is 80 years of labor compared to 1000 years?

Christian, yes, if you have been born again, then you are going to Heaven. You cannot lose your salvation. A preacher was rebuked for believing once saved, always saved. He replied, *"Well I just believe once born, always born."* So, yes, you are going to Heaven, but dear Christian, remember this, if the Lord came today and called us out of this world to be caught up together with Him in the air, then there is at least 1007 years before

The Sons of Zadok

the tears are wiped away. One day they will be wiped away, but 1007 years is a long time where it will be obvious whether you loved your Saviour, or whether you loved someone or something else more.

Chapter 5

The Christian

Ah, yes, it is now time to answer the question: What will you do for 1000 years?

You now understand where we are in the time frame. It is the last 1000 years of this present universe. That's right, this universe. For at the end of this 1000-year millennial reign of Jesus Christ, the universe is dissolved, which obviously includes this earth. It is a sobering thought. All that you and I see in our life time is going to burn up one day.

[10]But the day of the Lord will come as a thief in the night; in the which **the heavens shall pass away with a great noise, and the elements shall melt with fervent heat**, the earth also and the works that are therein shall be **burned up**.

[11]Seeing then *that* all these things shall be dissolved, what manner *of persons* ought ye

The Sons of Zadok

to be in *all* holy conversation and godliness, ¹²Looking for and hasting unto the coming of the day of God, wherein **the heavens being on fire shall be dissolved, and the elements shall melt with fervent heat?** (2 Pet. 3:10-12)

It is sad to realize that in this Laodicean period, so many Christians work very hard all of their lives for material things only to have them burn up. Not only that, but they work so hard for those things also, yet to miss out on having eternal treasures laid up in Heaven. And not only that, but they will lose their inheritance which is the privilege to reign with Jesus Christ for 1000 years. I may get a bit *"preachy"* in this chapter, but this is the point of the whole book. It is so important to realize what a Christian can lose in this regard.

As I write this book, we are in the Laodicean period, and it is a period that is marked by carnal physical possessions. The Christians use their possessions as evidence that they are right with God. **"Because thou sayest I am rich and increased with goods..."** (Rev 3:17). They are of the mindset of, **"...supposing that gain is godliness...** (1 Tim. 6:5). Yet the word of God says, **"...from such withdraw thyself"** (1 Tim. 6:5). That is a major disconnect! The average Laodicean Christian is convinced his possessions are evidence he is right with God. Yet the word of God commands you to get away from them. God also states, **"...and knowest not that thou art wretched, and miserable, and poor, and blind, and naked..."** (Rev 3:17). To be wretched is to be worse than simple poverty. It is to be as if living in the gutter, clothed in dirty rags and barefoot.

The Christian

This earthly physical life is not the time to reign, or to live as a king or queen. It is the time to serve and suffer.

Our Lord Jesus Christ is our greatest example of service and suffering. Yes, it is to be expected that he is our greatest example, but consider what he went through in His suffering.

Can you picture your Saviour nailed to an old rugged cross? On either side of him are two guilty men dying for their crimes, yet Jesus Christ was innocent. His flesh has been shredded from the scourge that had been slapped across His back, His body, His arms and His legs. Pieces of flesh hang outward from his body. Blood runs down and drips off His arms and legs, as well as running down the Cross. His beard has been ripped off of His cheeks and blood drips off His chin. Every bone is out of joint, yet not a single bone is broken. Can you imagine every bone being out of joint? His tongue cleaves to His jaws.

Then, in the darkness at noon, He is attacked by devils loosed from the pit of Hell. They attack Him with a vengeance. Though the angels are ready to come and deliver him, they are not allowed to do so. The Father watches, but sends no aid, no escape. In the darkness at Calvary Jesus is dying alone; he is fighting alone, and he is doing a great job, for the Bible says, "**...he made a show of them openly**" (Col. 2:15). The devils, the principalities, and powers were unable to gain the least bit of ground against the Son of God that day. He made a show of them openly, triumphing over them in it.

Then in the darkness, He cries out, "**...My God, My God, Why hast thou forsaken me?**" (Mark 15:34). All alone Jesus suffers, bleeds and dies on Calvary to pay for your sins, and to obey the Father's will. He paid the greatest price, and suffered the greatest agony, so therefore He ends up with the greatest position in the Millennium. He is the King of all the earth, as well as Heaven. *The greatest suffering brings the greatest reign.* Jesus is our greatest example of how we are to live now, and thus how we will live for 1000 years then.

We are now going to get into direct application. You are now reading what will happen to you. Notice the following verses:

> ^{11}*It is* a faithful saying: For if we be dead with *him*, we shall also live with *him*:
> ^{12}**If we suffer, we shall also reign with *him*: if we deny *him*, he also will deny us:**
> ^{13}If we believe not, *yet* he abideth faithful: he cannot deny himself. (2 Tim. 2:11-13)

In regards to verse 11. If you are born again, then you are dead with your Lord Jesus Christ. Paul writes,

> ^{20}**I am crucified with Christ:** nevertheless I live; yet not I, but Christ liveth in me: and the life which I now live in the flesh I live by the faith of the Son of God, who loved me, and gave himself for me. (Gal. 2:20)
> ^{3}...**Ye are dead,** and your life is hid with Christ in God. (Col. 3:3)

When you got saved, spiritually you were crucified with Jesus Christ. So you are going to live with Him, and actually you are living with Him right now for you are *"in Christ."*

Now, in regards to verse 2 Tim. 2:12. **"If we suffer..."** There is a lot in those three words. The word suffer is

The Christian

often associated with pain and sorrow, but that is not the only way the word is used. Jesus said,

> ^{14}But when Jesus saw *it*, he was much displeased, and said unto them, **Suffer the little children to come unto me**, and forbid them not: for of such is the kingdom of God. (Mark 10:14)

So the word *"suffer"* also has the meaning of "to permit or allow." **"If we suffer, we shall also reign with Him."** The context of this verse is the millennial reign of Jesus Christ when He lives on this earth for 1000 years. This is the only "reign" that can be denied to a Christian. In eternity with the new heavens and earth it is written:

> ^{17}For, behold, I create new heavens and a new earth: and **the former shall not be remembered, nor come into mind.** (Isa. 65:17)

There is coming a day when we will no longer remember this life. The only remaining thing in eternity to remind us will be the scars on the body of our Lord Jesus Christ, and they will remind us of His love for each one of us.

So, here in 2 Timothy 2:12 the reign is a reference to the millennial reign of Christ. In order to reign with Him then, you will have to suffer Jesus Christ to reign in your heart and life now. And that will bring pain and suffering into your life, no doubt.

If we suffer... is to submit to Jesus Christ. Instead of your will, you surrender and live according to God's will for your life. What does that mean? It means you line up your life with the word of God and God's will for your

141

The Sons of Zadok

life to the very best of your ability.

Are you living in the house God wants you to live in? Are you working at the job God wants you to work at? Are you in church? Are you tithing? Is there someone that you need to go apologize to? Regardless of social status or financial cost, is there something that you know God wants you to do? You had better do it while you can.

Are we perfect? No! Do we always do right? No! But it is your submission to the Lord, and repentance when you fail that God is looking for. Let me give you some examples.

In this age, old as well as young, Christians are living together and not getting married. They claim, *"But if we get married, we will lose some of our financial benefits."* So they *"shack up,"* live in sin, and lose out on their 1000-year inheritance.

In the winter time, the Lord has allowed Terri and me to rest for some weeks at our home church in southern Alabama. During this time we enjoy going down to the beach and walking. It is the only time of year when people have their clothes on, thus making it much more enjoyable and spiritually clean.

The Gulf Shores facility is very nice and has a parking lot. From there you can look out towards the ocean and watch the waves, listen to the sea gulls, and enjoy the ocean breeze. One time as we were walking back to our car, an older man and woman were sitting in a shiny clean, modern red Chevy truck. They had the windows down, and as we walked up, the man spoke up and asked where we were from. The conversation continued with small talk, and after a bit I asked him if he was

The Christian

saved. To this question he replied, "Yes," and that he was a member of the First Baptist church in Gulf Shores.

As the conversation proceeded, something was said about his wife, and he replied that they were not married, but they were living together. What is worse is that they were not ashamed at all and freely admitted it. There was no conviction about abstaining from all appearance of evil. There was no conviction about the need to get married so that they could have a good testimony. There was no concern about trying to be right before God.

Were they saved? Well, they said they were. If they are, they will lose out on their reigning with Jesus Christ in the Millennium.

> [5]For this ye know, that no whoremonger, nor unclean person, nor covetous man, who is an idolater, **hath any inheritance in the kingdom of Christ and of God.** (Eph. 5:5)

There are Christians whom God has called into a certain work for Him, but they are not going or doing because of the hardship. Thus they are not faithful to God's will for their life. They will lose their inheritance and not reign with Christ for 1000 years.

I know a lady, a very bitter, hard, rebellious lady. She is in her late 80's now. She confessed one day to my wife that when she was a young girl, the Lord Jesus Christ called her to the mission field, but she never went. So sad! The rebellious, selfish heart that kept her from obeying God's call was manifested in her rebellious bitter spirit when she was in church. She did not suffer the Lord to lead her, so she will not reign with

The Sons of Zadok

him either.

Perhaps you ask, *"Well, what will she do then?"* Honestly, I am not exactly sure, though there is one thing that is very sure, she will not reign with Christ. She wouldn't serve Him now, she will not reign with him then.

So I ask you dear reader: what does God want you to do now? He has a job that He wants you to do for Him. Do you know what it is? Maybe you go to church, tithe and even give above your tithe. Maybe you faithfully read your Bible and pray every day. That is good and right. But there is something that you know God wants you to do. It is coming to your mind as you read this. So what are you going to do? Are you going to suffer with Him, or are you going to rebel against Him? Yes, you will still go to Heaven, and yes you will still have a gold mansion, and yes, you will still have a new body one day. But if you do not suffer Jesus Christ to rule you now, then you will not reign with Him for 1000 years.

Maybe if you surrender to your Saviour, it will cost you your career, your house, and even your retirement. But will you surrender anyway? Will you let God be your Lord and Master?

"If we deny Him..." (2 Tim. 2:12). If you will not allow Jesus Christ to be your Lord and Master now, then He will not let you reign then. Basically you are saying to your Lord, *"I want to do what I want to do, when I want to do it, the way I want to do it."* You are denying the Lordship of your Saviour Jesus Christ. And He will deny you. No, He is not denying you of your salvation. Your salvation is fixed. In the context of 2 Tim. 2, Paul

The Christian

is referring to the millennial reign with Jesus Christ. You need to get your eyes off the present time and put them on the future.

In regards to verse 2 Tim. 2:13, **"If we believe not, *yet* he abideth faithful: he cannot deny himself."** Aren't you glad the Lord is faithful? In this age there are born again people all over the world who are not faithful to Jesus Christ. They are more interested in their personal comfort than obeying Him. But Jesus Christ is faithful to them. He cannot deny himself.

You see, when you were born again, you were baptized into the body of Jesus Christ. It was not a baptism by water but a baptism that was performed by the Holy Spirit when you were saved.

> [13]**For by one Spirit are we all baptized into one body**, whether *we be* Jews or Gentiles, whether *we be* bond or free; and have been **all made to drink into one Spirit.** (1 Cor. 12:13)
> [30]For we are members of his body, **of his flesh, and of his bones.** (Eph. 5:30)

If you were to lose your salvation, it would as if Jesus Christ lost part of His own body, and that is not going to happen. **"He cannot deny himself."** So, yes you are going to Heaven if you are born again. And maybe you are so carnal as to think, *"Well, at least I am not going to Hell."* But in the back of your mind something is gnawing at your conscience, and it is the Holy Spirit saying, *"Won't you obey me? I have a job for you to do."*

In this age most of the Christians just won't obey. They won't suffer with the Lord. And even some end up in trials to the point where they profess that there is no God. They believe not. But Jesus Christ abideth

The Sons of Zadok

faithful, and thank God that He does. One day though, there will be much regret.

Consider the story of the Prodigal Son. You see, both of the sons were born with an inheritance. It was theirs by birth.

If you are born again, you are given an inheritance at your spiritual birth. It is this 1000-year reign with Jesus Christ. You already know of the verses in 2 Tim. 2, but now consider the following:

> [16]The Spirit itself beareth witness with our spirit, that we are the children of God:
>
> [17]And if children, then heirs; heirs of God, and joint-heirs with Christ; **if so be that we suffer with *him*, that we may be also glorified together.**
>
> [18]For I reckon that the sufferings of this present time *are* not worthy *to be compared* with the glory which shall be revealed in us.
> (Rom. 8:16-18)

As a child of God then, you are an heir. An heir is someone who inherits either a title deed, or possessions. Notice it says, **"joint-heirs with Christ."** Wow! Think about that! Your salvation was free, but along with it you became an heir of God. A joint-heir with Christ.

We covered the inheritance already, but just to remind you of that inheritance. Concerning the Jews it is the physical land in Israel, but for the Christian it is the reigning with Jesus Christ over this earth for 1000 years. Jesus Christ will reign from the Holy oblation in the midst of Israel. (Eze 48:21)

> [10]And for them, even for the priests, shall be

this holy oblation; toward the north five and twenty thousand in length, and toward the west ten thousand in breadth, and toward the east ten thousand in breadth, and toward the south five and twenty thousand in length: and **the sanctuary of the LORD shall be in the midst thereof.**

^{21}And the residue shall be **for the prince**, on the one side and on the other of the holy oblation, and of the possession of the city, over against the five and twenty thousand of the oblation toward the east border, and westward over against the five and twenty thousand toward the west border, over against the portions for the prince: and it shall be the holy oblation; and **the sanctuary of the house shall be in the midst thereof.** (Ezek. 48:10, 21)

^{31}When the Son of man shall come in his glory, and all the holy angels with him, then shall **he sit upon the throne of his glory:** (Matt. 25:31)

The throne of His glory will be in the sanctuary of the Lord, which is in the midst of the holy oblation.

Romans 8:17 declares that you/we are, **"...joint heirs with Christ..."** but then there is an ominous warning very similar to what was written in 2 Timothy. Notice the qualification that is attached to being joint-heirs with Christ. **"...if so be that we suffer with him..."** (Rom 8:17). So being a joint-heir with Christ, and your inheritance being the 1000-year reign with Christ on this earth, you must suffer with Him now. Are you suffering your Lord to run your life? Have you given Him the steering wheel? Is God your Pilot, or is He merely your co-Pilot?

It shouldn't matter what you will lose if you surrender to the Lord's will for your life. If you got what you deserve, you would be in Hell right now. "**...what hast thou that thou didst not receive?**" (1 Cor. 4:7). It's time you gave Jesus Christ the steering wheel and took your hands off your own will and life. There is an inheritance that you are getting ready to lose if you don't submit to your Lord Jesus Christ and His will for your life.

The Lord has every right to refuse you your inheritance if you do not suffer Him to rule you now. Here is the King of the universe, Jesus Christ. He has holes in His hands, His feet and His side from when He gave His life, shed his blood, and died to saved your unworthy soul from Hell. You come as you are, filthy, deserving of Hell, and ask for forgiveness, and He forgives and saves you.

Then the King of the universe touches you and says, *"I have a job that I would like you to do for me,"* and you say, *"**No! I don't want to do that!**"*

As they say in New York, **"What, ah ya crazy?!"** But so many saints do that very thing and tell the Lord, **"No!"** You need to realize that the value of a thing is based upon the cost. So too, the value of your Christianity is based upon what it cost you. The Lord said to buy of him, "**...gold tried in the fire, that thou mayest be rich...**" (Rev. 3:18). That is a command, not a suggestion. To buy of Him means that there is a cost. It is going to have to cost you something in order to get the true gold and to not remain wretched.

Your inheritance is contingent upon you suffering

The Christian

with Jesus Christ now, according to 2 Timothy, and Romans 8.

^{23}And whatsoever ye do, do *it* heartily, as to the Lord, and not unto men;

^{24}Knowing that of the Lord ye shall receive **the reward of the inheritance:** for ye serve the Lord Christ.

^{25}But **he that doeth wrong shall receive for the wrong which he hath done:** and there is no respect of persons. (Col. 3:23-25)

In verse 24, your inheritance is said to be a **"reward."** As a child of God you are born with an inheritance, which is reigning with Jesus Christ on this earth for 1000 years. But it is a reward and therefore can be lost. Will you have your reward and reign with Jesus Christ, or will you receive for the wrong which you have done?

It is so wrong to tell your Saviour no! You may not have said that with your mouth, but your works are the evidence that you have said "no" in your heart. This brings us to the story in the word of God and it is a very famous story. It is the story of the Prodigal Son.

^{11}And he said, A certain man had two sons:

^{12}And the younger of them said to *his* father, Father, *give me* the portion of goods that falleth to *me*. And he divided unto them his living.

^{13}And not many days after the younger son gathered all together, and took his journey into a far country, and there wasted his substance with riotous living.

^{14}And when he had spent all, there arose a mighty famine in that land; and he began to

The Sons of Zadok

be in want.

^{15}And he went and joined himself to a citizen of that country; and he sent him into his fields to feed swine.

^{16}And he would fain have filled his belly with the husks that the swine did eat: and no man gave unto him.

^{17}And when he came to himself, he said, How many hired servants of my father's have bread enough and to spare, and I perish with hunger!

^{18}I will arise and go to my father, and will say unto him, Father, I have sinned against heaven, and before thee,

^{19}And am no more worthy to be called thy son: **make me as one of thy hired servants.**

^{20}And he arose, and came to his father. But when he was yet a great way off, his father saw him, and had compassion, and ran, and fell on his neck, and kissed him.

^{21}And the son said unto him, Father, I have sinned against heaven, and in thy sight, and am no more worthy to be called thy son.

^{22}But the father said to his servants, Bring forth the best robe, and put *it* on him; and put a ring on his hand, and shoes on *his* feet:

^{23}And bring hither the fatted calf, and kill *it*; and let us eat, and be merry:

^{24}For this **my son was dead,** and is alive again; he was lost, and is found. And they began to be merry.

^{25}Now his elder son **was in the field:** and as

The Christian

he came and drew nigh to the house, he heard musick and dancing.

^{26}And he called one of the servants, and asked what these things meant.

^{27}And he said unto him, Thy brother is come; and thy father hath killed the fatted calf, because he hath received him safe and sound.

^{28}And he was angry, and would not go in: therefore came his father out, and intreated him.

^{29}And he answering said to *his* father, Lo, these many years do I serve thee, neither transgressed I at any time thy commandment: and yet thou never gavest me a kid, that I might make merry with my friends:

^{30}But as soon as this thy son was come, which hath devoured thy living with harlots, thou hast killed for him the fatted calf.

^{31}And he said unto him, Son, **thou art ever with me, and all that I have is thine.**

^{32}It was meet that we should make merry, and be glad: for this thy brother **was dead,** and is alive again; and was lost, and is found. (Luke 15:11-32)

    The hero of this story is the father who is thrilled that his son has come home. His love for his son is obvious as he holds a great celebration because his son has returned home. To the father, when his younger son was gone away, it was as if he were dead. He is a picture of our Heavenly Father who is loving and forgiving as well. I am sure we have no idea just how great the love of our Heavenly Father is for us. Yet, just as the father of the Prodigal Son considered him as dead, when he was in the far away country, so too, there is a similar experience with the born again saint.

^{13}**For if ye live after the flesh, ye shall die:** but if ye through the Spirit do mortify the deeds of the body, ye shall live. (Rom. 8:13)
^{14}Wherefore he saith, Awake thou that sleepest, and **arise from the dead,** and Christ shall give thee light. (Eph. 5:14)

A Christian who lives after the flesh spiritually dies. And it doesn't take long for it to happen. All you have to do is give up and do whatever your flesh desires to do. You start living after the flesh, and before you know it, you are dead.

It is obviously not physical death because in Ephesians 5:14, it says to **"arise from the dead, And Christ shall give thee light."** It's time to wake up! Are you spiritually dead?

To his father, the Prodigal Son was dead, but now he was alive again. It is a great picture of a carnal Christian who repents and gets right with God. The repentance of the Prodigal is a very important element to his return home. He is now willing to be a servant. Repentance is required in order to get right with God. Repentance is required in order to be reconciled to God.

Then there is the older son in this story. Often times the older son is heavily rebuked by both preachers and Bible teachers for his attitude. But there are some very important things to notice about the older son in this

The Christian

story.

First of all, it is to be expected that the older son would be a little upset; for he had done his father right and never transgressed him at any time. Why should there be a celebration for his younger brother who had wasted his inheritance? So, too, there are Christians who have served God faithfully all of their saved life. And then there are the Christians who have wasted their lives trying to make money, getting material things, and-or, seeking earthly popularity.

So, both groups of Christians will live eternally in Heaven. Both of them will have a golden mansion. Both of them are in the bride of Christ and will be married to Jesus Christ one day. Both of them will have perfect, glorified bodies one day. So, just as I introduced this book, *"If God is going to wipe away all tears from our eyes one day, then why are we trying so hard?"*

Because there are rewards to be gained and an inheritance to be given to those who are faithful in their service for their Lord Jesus Christ. Notice what the father says to the elder son.

First thing the father says is, "**...Son, thou art ever with me.**" (vs 31) Did you get that? But the elder son had been out in the field working, getting sweaty and dirty. Right? He had not been at home with the father. The implication here is that his working days are over. He will now be at home with his father.

Do you remember the priests about which the Lord said, "**They'll not come near me...?**" Yes, those are

The Sons of Zadok

Jews, but for the Christian it is this.

At the start of the Millennium the Lord is going to be giving out the reward of the inheritance. It will be in the form of reigning with Jesus Christ over cities. You will have a perfect body, and you will fully love your Saviour because your corrupt flesh is no longer a part of you. You will *"automatically"* do right. If you did not live for, and love Jesus Christ the way you should have, then at this time in your saved life you will.

As your Lord is giving out the reward of the inheritance, you are going to see the city that you were to have to reign over. With excitement you may step forward to claim it, when the Lord puts forth His hand and stops you. No! You didn't serve me and lived after the flesh. No, give that city to so-and-so, who was faithful. You will know the Lord is right and all you can do is hang your head in shame.

Does He love you? Yes, just as the father of the Prodigal loved him. Now notice the next thing the father says to the elder son.

"And all that I have is thine" (vs 31). Did you get that? There was nothing left in the estate for the younger son. He had spent it all. Again, the implication is that the younger son was going to go to work, as a servant. How far the type can be applied, I do not know. Will an unfaithful Christian have to work for 1000 years? I don't know. But I do know this. The reason born again people do not serve the Lord Jesus Christ is because of pride, selfishness, or they are ashamed of the Lord. During the Millennium, the fact that you are not

The Christian

reigning over a city will testify openly that you did not love Him enough to live for Him now. *You need to think about that!*

You may be discouraged. You may be at the end of your strength. You may not know how you are going to make it through the storm that you are in. But do not quit in your heart. Do not turn your back on Jesus Christ. "...having done all to stand. Stand therefore..." (Eph 6:13-14). Maybe all you can do is lie on the floor or ground, and cry. (I have been there.) Yes, but don't turn your back on Jesus Christ. Pray for grace and mercy, for it is grace and mercy that you need.

With the grace of God, you are able to endure the trials that God allows to come your way. I write this knowing that I am writing of things greater than I understand, but know them to be so. Consider the following two amazing, supernatural, yet true stories taken from Foxe's Book of Martyrs:

> Thomas Haukes, with six others, was condemned on the ninth of February, 1555. In education he was erudite; in person, comely, and of good stature; in manners, a gentleman, and a sincere Christian. A little before death, several of Mr. Hauke's friends, terrified by the sharpness of the punishment he was going to suffer, privately desired that in the midst of the flames he should show them some token, whether the pains of burning were so great that a man might not collectedly endure it. This he

The Sons of Zadok

promised to do; and it was agreed that if the rage of the pain might be suffered, then he should lift up his hands above his head towards heaven, before he gave up the ghost.

Not long after, Mr. Haukes was led away to the place appointed for slaughter by Lord Rich, and being come to the stake, mildly and patiently prepared himself for the fire, having a strong chain cast about his middle, with a multitude of people on every side compassing him about, unto whom after he had spoken many things, and poured out his soul unto God, the fire was kindled.

When he had continued long in it, and his speech was taken away by violence of the flame, his skin drawn together, and his fingers consumed with the fire, so that it was thought that he was gone, suddenly and contrary to all expectation, this good man being mindful of his promise, reached up his hands burning in flames over his head to the living God, and with great rejoicings as it seemed, struck or clapped them three times together. A great shout followed this wonderful circumstance, and then this blessed martyr of Christ, sinking down in the fire, gave up his spirit, June 10, 1555.

Dr. John Hooper - Pastor 1554

About eight o'clock, on February 9, 1555, he was led forth, and many thousand persons

The Christian

were collected, as it was market-day. All the way, being straitly charged not to speak, and beholding the people, who mourned bitterly for him, he would sometimes lift up his eyes towards heaven, and look very cheerfully upon such as he knew: and he was never known, during the time of his being among them, to look with so cheerful and ruddy a countenance as he did at that time. When he came to the place appointed where he should die, he smilingly beheld the stake and preparation made for him, which was near unto the great elm tree over against the college of priests, where he used to preach.

Now, after he had entered into prayer, a box was brought and laid before him upon a stool, with his pardon from the queen, if he would turn. At the sight whereof he cried, "If you love my soul, away with it!" The box being taken away, Lord Chandois said, "Seeing there is no remedy; despatch him quickly."

Command was now given that the fire should be kindled. But because there were not more green fagots than two horses could carry, it kindled not speedily, and was a pretty while also before it took the reeds upon the fagots. At length it burned about him, but the wind having full strength at that place, and being a lowering cold morning, it blew the flame from him, so that he was in a manner little more than touched by the fire.

Within a space after, a few dry fagots were brought, and a new fire kindled with fagots, (for there were no more reeds) and those burned at the nether parts, but had small power above, because of the wind, saving that it burnt his hair and scorched his skin a little. In the time of which fire, even as at the first flame, he prayed, saying mildly, and not very loud, but as one without pain, "O Jesus, Son of David, have mercy upon me, and receive my soul!" After the second fire was spent, he wiped both his eyes with his hands, and beholding the people, he said with an indifferent, loud voice, "For God's love, good people, let me have more fire!" and all this while his nether parts did burn; but the fagots were so few that the flame only singed his upper parts.

The third fire was kindled within a while after, which was more extreme than the other two. In this fire he prayed with a loud voice, "Lord Jesus, have mercy upon me! Lord Jesus receive my spirit!" And these were the last words he was heard to utter. But when he was black in the mouth, and his tongue so swollen that he could not speak, yet his lips went until they were shrunk to the gums: and he knocked his breast with his hands until one of his arms fell off, and then knocked still with the other, while the fat, water, and blood dropped out at

The Christian

his fingers' ends, until by renewing the fire, his strength was gone, and his hand clave fast in knocking to the iron upon his breast. Then immediately bowing forwards, he yielded up his spirit.

Thus was he three quarters of an hour or more in the fire. Even as a lamb, patiently he abode the extremity thereof, neither moving forwards, backwards, nor to any side; but he died as quietly as a child in his bed. And he now reigneth, I doubt not, as a blessed martyr in the joys of heaven, prepared for the faithful in Christ before the foundations of the world; for whose constancy all Christians are bound to praise God.

The faithfulness of those two saints, Hooper and Haukes, is a grand testimony of how we ought to be. It is also a rebuke when you begin to murmur and complain about how rough you have it. If they remained faithful in their fiery trials, then you and I can remain faithful in our "fiery" trials. But let me give you a "heads up" concerning the age in which we live.

There is some blatant persecution happening as I write this book in 2022. Christians are being beat in places around the world. Some are getting their heads cut off from what I have read. I am not in any way minimizing their suffering. But for the most part, Christians, especially American Christians, in this age are loaded with money and things. The temptation

The Sons of Zadok

today is to seek material riches instead of serving and living for Jesus Christ.

So, while most of us are not being persecuted, yet there is a vast selling out, and compromising with the world in order to keep physical junk. Don't do it! Make sure, you are diligent to put Jesus Christ and His will for your life, first. I know I have already written this, and forgive me for writing it again: if you will lose a house, money, things and whatever else you have because you submit to God's will for your life, do it anyway. Amen! Don't let the materialism of this age ruin you.

My wife and I, had already lived in various places, slept on floors, lived in trailers with mice and rats coming through the floor and in the cupboards. We had been homeless and allowed to sleep on the floor of a mobile home from a compassionate brother in the Lord. It was his home, and he had two children and a wife as well.

When I surrendered to the call of evangelism we had finally moved into a modern, three bedroom, two bath home. The home was in the mountains of California. The area was where I grew up, and it is a very beautiful area. The house was a new build. It was clean, it had a wood stove, I planted a garden and we "throughly" enjoyed it. We had been living there for about three years when I realized God wanted me in evangelism. The Lord was very gracious to us as He gave us plenty of leading and assurance that He wanted me in the field of evangelism.

My first two meetings were in Texas, and I was able

The Christian

to use my two weeks of vacation to go and preach. It was my trial run, and all went well. My next outing was three months, and then it went to nine months, and then full-time.

Then it came time that we had to sell the house. When you have been homeless, it is not easy to sell your house. But God sold it in two weeks. The first eight years in evangelism, we lived out of a car. But by the grace of God we stayed faithful and are still preaching to this day. Even as I write this in 2022, my wife and I are living out of a 1994 motorhome, and we have no permanent/stationary dwelling. But we have food and raiment, and with that we are content.

^{12}Wherefore let him that thinketh he standeth take heed lest he fall.

^{13}There hath no temptation taken you but such as is common to man: but God *is* faithful, who will not suffer you to be tempted above that ye are able; but will with the temptation also make a way to escape, that ye may be able to bear *it*.

^{14}Wherefore, my dearly beloved, **flee from idolatry**. (1 Cor. 10:12-14)

There are many others today who are living in much worse accommodations and have little to nothing, because they have stepped out by faith and obeyed God's will for their life. They are faithful to God's will for their life. Are you?

Maybe you have many material possessions, and you are right in the will of God, serving Him faithfully.

The Sons of Zadok

Amen! That is good. Poverty is not a mark of being right with God. But materialism is a mark of Laodicea. And while the temptation today may not be the threat of being burnt at the stake, yet the temptation today is very subtle and very real. It is the temptation to keep your things at the expense of serving Jesus Christ.

Will you be faithful? God is not interested in you being successful. It is His will for you to be faithful to His perfect will for your life. If you are faithful to God's will for your life, then you will be rewarded. One of those rewards is to reign with Jesus Christ in the Millennium for 1000 years.

The faithful Christian will be given cities to reign over, and at least once a year they will take people over to Jerusalem to worship the Lord Jesus Christ. This is a must do. No Christian will refuse to go, and no Christian will refuse to bring his city.

But those who do not go once a year, to worship the King, then on their land will be no rain. And if they still do not go worship the Lord then they will be hit with a plague.

> ^{16}And it shall come to pass, *that* every one that is left of all the nations which came against Jerusalem shall even go up from year to year to worship the King, the LORD of hosts, and to keep the feast of tabernacles.
>
> ^{17}And it shall be, *that* whoso will not come up of *all* the families of the earth unto Jerusalem to worship the King, the LORD of hosts, even **upon them shall be no rain.**

The Christian

¹⁸And if the family of Egypt go not up, and come not, that *have* no *rain*; there shall be the plague, wherewith the LORD will smite the heathen that come not up to keep the feast of tabernacles.

¹⁹This shall be the punishment of Egypt, and the punishment of all nations that come not up to keep the feast of tabernacles. (Zech. 14:16-19)

If you have a city to reign over, how are you going to transport your people over to Jerusalem? Would it be by airplane? I don't think so, but I'm not sure even of that. I don't know how the people will be transported, but I know that they will. If it is *your city,* then you will be leading the way and bringing them to see and worship the Lord Jesus Christ.

This now brings us to one last story in the word of God that applies to a Christian, and what they will do in the Millennium. It is found in Luke 19. It is the parable of the pounds.

¹²He said therefore, A certain **nobleman** went into a far country **to receive for himself a kingdom, and to return.**

¹³And he called his **ten servants,** and delivered them **ten pounds,** and said unto them, Occupy till I come.

¹⁴But his citizens hated him, and sent a message after him, saying, We will not have this *man* to reign over us.

¹⁵And it came to pass, that when he was

returned, **having received the kingdom,** then he commanded these servants to be called unto him, to whom he had given the money, that he might know how much every man had gained **by trading.**

[16]Then came the first, saying, Lord, **thy pound hath gained ten pounds.**

[17]And he said unto him, Well, thou good servant: because thou hast been faithful in a very little, **have thou authority over ten cities.**

[18]And the second came, saying, **Lord, thy pound hath gained five pounds.**

[19]And he said likewise to him, **Be thou also over five cities.**

[20]And another came, saying, Lord, behold, *here is* thy pound, which I have kept **laid up in a napkin:**

[21]For I feared thee, because thou art an austere man: thou takest up that thou layedst not down, and reapest that thou didst not sow.

[22]And he saith unto him, Out of thine own mouth will I judge thee, *thou* wicked servant. Thou knewest that I was an austere man, taking up that I laid not down, and reaping that I did not sow:

[23]Wherefore then gavest not thou my money into the bank, that at my coming I might have required mine own with usury?

^{24}And he said unto them that stood by, **Take from him the pound, and give** *it* **to him that hath ten pounds.**
^{25}(And they said unto him, Lord, he hath ten pounds.)
^{26}For I say unto you, **That unto every one which hath shall be given; and from him that hath not, even that he hath shall be taken away from him.** (Luke 19:12-26)

In this story the nobleman obviously pictures our Lord Jesus Christ. His citizens would be Gentile, for Jesus Christ though rejected by Jews, was crucified by Roman Gentiles. The kingdom is His millennial reign that takes place when our Lord returns to this earth the second time. He calls ten servants and gives each of them ten pounds along with a command to occupy until He comes.

This story is not the same as the story that is found in Matthew 25. In Matthew 25 they are given talents which is a Jewish designation, and here in Luke they are given pounds which is an English, or Gentile, designation. The number 10 in the word of God has to do with the Gentiles whereas 12 has to do with Israel. In Matthew they are given various amounts, whereas here in Luke, they are all given the same amount: that being one pound.

You see, in the Church Age we all start at the same place. We are all sinners deserving of Hell. We all start out at salvation by being born again. At that point we begin to run a race for our Lord Jesus Christ.

The Sons of Zadok

I don't know if you have ever thought about this, but some Christians are very smart, or rich, or poor, or talented, while others have not so much talent. Abilities vary from person to person. Many times God's people feel unable, or intimidated, when it comes to doing something for their Lord Jesus Christ. But you must remember something very important. The Lord looks on your heart. Intelligence, ability, strength, and all the various qualities one person has or doesn't have is not what the Lord looks at. After all, Jesus did say that without Him "**...ye can do nothing.**" (Jn 15:15)

But there is a place where the ground is level. A place where no one is any better or worse than the other, and that place is the heart. It is the heart where you become willing, serving, and faithful to your Lord Jesus Christ. No amount of talent, or lack of talent, has an effect upon your heart. No amount of intelligence or lack of intelligence has any effect upon your heart. When it come to ability, we are all equal, for it all begins with your heart. So these servants in Luke 19 are all given the same measure, a pound.

It is interesting also that he gives ten servants a talent, but when he returns there are only three that he deals with, and out of those three only two have done right. Can it be that only 20 percent of all Christians actually serve the Lord?

I mentioned this to a man who works for the United Parcel Service, and without hesitation he replied: *"Yep, that's right. They have told us at UPS that 20 percent of the workers do all the work."* I have seen this in

The Christian

churches as well. It is just the faithful few that do the work in the church and ministry. Are you going to be one of those 20 percenters? By God's grace I want to be!

So the nobleman comes back and begins to take account of his servants. And there is something that is very, very important to notice in this story. *The ones who tried, gained.* The ones who tried, had an increase from the single pound that was given them. This is so instructive! Will you at least try? The other eight servants didn't even try.

The first one gains ten pounds. He has the joy of hearing his master say to him, **"Well, thou good servant: because thou hast been faithful in a very little, have thou authority over ten cities."** Oh to hear my Lord say, **"Well, thou good servant."** That alone is worth it all. To know that my Lord is pleased with me is my heart's highest desire. But also notice the reward, **"Have thou authority over ten cities."**

In this story the nobleman has returned, having received the kingdom. He is getting ready to reign over his kingdom. So he is giving out cities to reign over to those servants that were faithful. In this life as a Christian we are often being told what to do. This life now is to be a life of serving others.

> [28]**Even as the Son of man came not to be ministered unto, but to minister, and to give his life a ransom for many.** (Matt. 20:28)

Just as Jesus came the first time to minister and to give His life, so too in this earthly life of ours, it is our

The Sons of Zadok

duty to serve our Lord Jesus Christ first as well as others. We are to be last in our service, yet very few ever do this. You must realize that your attempt at serving your Lord will gain you the privilege of reigning with Jesus Christ for 1000 years. He will give you a city or more to reign over during that time. You know, the thought of reigning over cities and telling others what to do is a very pleasant thought to me.

So this first servant gains ten pounds by trading. In trading you must give it away. Of course there are the trades, such as carpenters, plumbers, electricians, and so on. They give their time and ability away for the return of money. But this pound is to be traded for the master, and if you will try, then you will gain. No maybe, might or possibly—you will gain! The ones that tried, gained and were rewarded with authority over cities.

The other faithful servant gained five pounds and was given authority over five cities.

Now, here is another thing to think about. The United States of America, for example, is almost 250 years old. When Columbus discovered America, that was a little over 500 years ago, and there were a few hundred thousand Mongolians living here. That's right, they are Mongolians. They came over through Alaska probably, and the Europeans came across the Atlantic. Neither were native to America, but that is another subject.

So 500 years ago, there were a few hundred thousand people living on this continent, and during that time there were lions, tigers and bears...oh my! Why do I say

The Christian

that? Because those wild animals were attacking and eating humans at times. Along with that, there were plagues, diseases, and deadly weather. And on top of that there were wars upon wars. Europeans and Mongolians were fighting and killing each other. There was the Revolutionary War, the Civil War, World War 1, and World War 2, Korean War, Viet Nam War, Desert Storm, and so on. And during these 500 years, despite the people that were killed, as of 2022, just in the USA, there are approximately 332 million people living in this country.

So now imagine it is the Millennium, and you are given a city or two. And let's suppose your city is a wide spot in the road with a gas station, a post office and a store. Well during this reign of Jesus Christ, the people will live like they did in Genesis, so people will live to be around 700 or 800 years old.

> [20]There shall be no more thence an infant of days, nor an old man that hath not filled his days: for **the child shall die an hundred years old;** (Isa. 65:20)

There is death in the Millennium, but notice a child is said to be 100 years old. (I wonder how old those children are in the streets of Jerusalem? I would guess just a few years old, but it doesn't say.) So here you have this little city. Do you realize how big your city will be in just a few hundred years? It will be much, much larger than New York City. One of the largest metropolitan areas on earth is Tokyo, Japan, with over 37.4,000,000 people.

The Sons of Zadok

(https://populationstat.com/japan/tokyo)

But your cities will dwarf that in just a few hundred years in the Millennium.

In the Millennium, child birth might be painless, the same as it was in the Garden of Eden. But even if it is not, yet it will be much easier than now. Women will have children for many, many years, for their body and health will be excellent. I would imagine also that to have children will be a joy, and never a burden. Life, and birth, will truly be an enjoyable glorious thing.

With Jesus Christ on the throne, there will be no whining of population control or the need to preserve the earth. The earth will be in its regeneration and thus beautiful beyond compare. There will be no food shortages whatsoever. It is going to be a glorious time indeed. And if you are faithful now, you will be given cities then to reign over. Those cities will be enormous after a few hundred years, let alone by 900 years. Your city could easily have over a billion people in it. And you will have the authority over that city, if...if...if you will at least try to serve Him now.

Is there something that you know the Lord wants you to do for Him? You had best get busy doing it. It doesn't matter if you have to sell your house, lose all your money, and step out by faith. Now is not the time to reign, now is the time to take your pound and trade it. When the King returns, then you will reign with Him.

Not only do the faithful get cities, but did you notice the one servant that buried his lord's pound? What happened? His pound was taken from him and given

The Christian

to him that had ten pounds. I wonder where the other seven pounds ended up? There were seven other servants that were each given a pound, and it appears from the story that they did not do anything with their pounds either.

The implications are outstanding. If you will try to serve the Lord now by trading and working for Him, then you will be given cities to reign over; also you will be given cities that are taken from the unfaithful and given to you. Wow!

But now, think about this. Here you are, and you have not served your Lord Jesus Christ in this life. Your service and your efforts were to get a house of your own and to make money, so that you will have a good retirement. And though you went to church, tithed, and prayed when called upon in church, yet your strength and labor was not in the work of the Lord. It was for physical things in this life.

No, you were not a bad person. Actually you were a model citizen. You loved your family and provided, or as a mother you took care of your husband and children. You did right, got saved and lived a clean life. But you did not put Jesus Christ first. He had a job He wanted you to do for Him. He asked you to step out by faith and serve Him, but you never did. You never went and did whatever your Lord asked or wanted you to do.

Well, here you are now at the beginning of the Millennium, and the Lord is giving out cities. He calls you forward to give you your inheritance.

Now, you have a new body, so you automatically love

The Sons of Zadok

your Lord Jesus Christ. There is no depraved flesh to fight you any more. Your love for the Lord is unfettered by sin and flesh. As you approach Him, your heart leaps for joy for your Saviour Jesus Christ. And somehow before you is presented a city, a place that was to be given you as a reward for your inheritance. But as you move to take it, the Lord stops you. With astonishment you stop and look at Him, and then hear Him say, *"Take from him and give to him over there."* And you watch as your inheritance is given to someone else. Will there be tears? Certainly! The tears are not wiped away until after the Millennium.

Perhaps when it comes time for the Millennium, you end up getting what you want. Have you ever thought about that? Would your Lord be unjust in giving you what you want? Oh, but in the 1000-year reign your heart is now right with God. The physical things of earth mean nothing anymore; after all, you don't need them now, do you? With your new body, you're never tired, sick, poor, or lonely.

With your new body you will love the Lord perfectly. But the opportunity to show the Lord you love Him is gone. You will love Him perfectly in your new body, and He loves and will love you. It's just that it is now manifest that you did not love Him enough to sacrifice and serve Him in this life. I guess, if you are ashamed of the Lord now in this life, you may be ashamed of yourself for 1000 years in the Millennium. Indeed it will be obvious if you loved the Lord or not.

But what if the Lord gives you what you wanted and

The Christian

what you worked for in this life? Let's say that you labored and worked for a house. As I travel the roads of America and the world, I see people in houses. Many of the houses in America are very large and very nice. But to get those houses, both parents usually work. Their lives (physical) and Labors (physical) are wrapped up around the house (physical), their retirement (physical), and having a good time (physical). Many Christians live no different than their next door atheistic neighbor.

So you watch as your city is given to someone who was faithful (spiritual) in this life. Perhaps tears well up in your eyes as you realize the Lord is right. Then you look up at him and ask, *"Lord, what do I get?"* What if the Lord says to you, *"You can go get a house; after all, that is all you wanted isn't it?"*

> [24] **No man can serve two masters:** for either he will hate the one, and love the other; or else he will hold to the one, and despise the other. **Ye cannot serve God and mammon.** (Matt. 6:24)

Is it a sin to have a house? Absolutely not! If that house is obtained after you have put Jesus Christ first, and after you have pursued God's perfect will for your life. If God allows you to have a house, then praise the Lord. But so many saints have things backwards. The house and retirement come before God's will for their life.

I remember staying in the house of a bank manager one time, and it was a very nice house. I heard him say

The Sons of Zadok

that in only a few more years he was going to retire, and then he wanted to get out and serve the Lord.

Well, the time came, and he retired. Not long after he retired and got the time to serve the Lord, he got sick and died.

God is not interested in your service for Him on your time table, and without any sacrifice. To serve the Lord supported by yourself is not something the Lord Jesus Christ is interested in. He wants you to step out by faith, when He calls you to, and *trust Him* for your provision. So many will not do this.

> ^{24}And after certain days, when Felix came with his wife Drusilla, which was a Jewess, he sent for Paul, and heard him concerning the faith in Christ.
> ^{25}And as he reasoned of righteousness, temperance, and judgment to come, Felix trembled, and answered, Go thy way for this time; **when I have a convenient season, I will call for thee.** (Acts 24:24-25)

The convenient season never came for Felix, and the convenient season will never come for you to serve the Lord. You must love and trust the Lord enough to step out by faith and do the work that God wants you to do. Will you trade? Will you try? It is God that gives the increase, not you.

What you do for 1000 years depends upon what you do for Him now. One thing is certain which is this, if you do not suffer with him now, you will not reign with him then. Comparing yourself with other Christians is

The Christian

not the way to judge how you are doing. What you must determine is if you are in God's perfect will for your life, and you are doing exactly what your Lord wants you to do. Otherwise you will not reign with Him for 1000 years.

If you are a wife whose husband is not surrendered to the Lord's will, then you can pray for him to surrender. And Sister, you had better be genuine in your surrender, for the Lord may answer your prayers. You may end up living out of a car, and sleeping on floors with snow falling on you.

For 1000 years it will be obvious how much you loved Jesus Christ in this life. It will be made manifest for all to see.

There are three offices in the word of God that a Christian ought to fulfill. They are a prophet, a priest and a king.

As a priest you have direct access to God. You do not go through a man. Jesus Christ opened the way and the veil was rent in twain. The Throne of Grace is open to you and available the moment you were born again. If you are saved, whether you are male or female, you are a priest.

The second office is that of a prophet. Rev. 19:10 says that, "**...the testimony of Jesus is the spirit of prophecy.**" As a Christian you are able to tell the future. For instance, you know where you are going when you die. The lost don't know this. Not only that, but you know where someone is going to go when they die if they are not saved. You know that. If you read and believe your King James Bible, then there are many, many things about the future that you know. You are a prophet.

But will you be a king? No, we are not to be kings now. Paul wrote:

> [8]Now ye are full, now ye are rich, ye have reigned as kings without us: and **I would to God ye did reign, that we also might reign with you.** (1 Cor. 4:8)

If we were reigning, then the suffering would be over. But we are not reigning now, and thus now is the time to suffer with the Lord. **If ye suffer ye shall reign. If ye deny him, he will deny you.**

So what is a king if he does not have a kingdom? Will you have a kingdom in the Millennium, or will you not? If not, then what will you do for 1000 years? Well, you won't reign over any cities. That much is clear.

I was talking to a man at church some years ago. This man traveled and sold books in churches. As we talked, we got on the subject of the Millennium. He told me that the Christians who are not faithful now will be cast into outer darkness where there shall be weeping, wailing and gnashing of teeth.

I looked at him and said, **"No way! That is not going to happen."** But he was adamant that yes, he believed they would be in outer darkness. So if you ever come across this heresy, remember this:

> [17]Then we which are alive and remain shall be caught up together with them in the clouds, to meet the Lord in the air: and **so**

The Christian

shall we ever be with the Lord. (1 Th. 4:17)

At the Rapture, which all who are born again shall be present in, we arise to meet the Lord in the air. And so shall we ever be with our Lord. If you were cast into outer darkness, you would not be with your Lord; the word of God states, "so shall we ever be with the Lord." Believe it!

Not only that, but if you are born again, then you are part of His bride whom He loves. He will not cast part of His bride and body into outer darkness.

Where do they get such a crazy doctrine? It comes from not rightly dividing the word of truth. They take Matthew 25, which has a Jewish, Tribulation application doctrinally, and they apply it to the Gentile church. This is why I went over the differences in the two stories earlier. In Matthew the unprofitable servant goes to Hell i.e. outer darkness where there is weeping and gnashing of teeth. In Luke the unprofitable servant DOES NOT go to Hell. Hence a church age application with eternal security.

> ^{30}And cast ye the unprofitable servant into outer darkness: there shall be **weeping and gnashing of teeth.** (Matt. 25:30)

Earlier in the Matt. 25 you have five virgins that are unwise and told to go out and buy oil for their lamps. That is works. Then at the end of the chapter, you have a man go to Hell because he didn't help Jews. This application is during the Tribulation. If you take Matthew 25 and apply it to the Church age, then you will end up with no eternal security, having to endure

The Sons of Zadok

unto the end, and thus a real doctrinal mess. For those who do not rightly divide the scriptures but do believe salvation is by grace through faith, then they must spiritualize the passage, for it is impossible for them to take it literally. And you may get some profitable lessons by spiritualizing the passage, but you will not be able to take it literally and thus doctrinally.

I met a man some years ago. He was slightly crippled but could walk, work, and function well on his own. He loved the Lord and lived a simple life collecting scrap metal. He memorized the Bible and was a faithful witness wherever he was; God used him in church and on the streets. One day, as we talked he told me his story.

He had been married to a saved lady and they had two children. She worked in the Christian school at the church where they were members. He was happy, and being a hardworking man, he provided a nice home and land for his family. But one day something very hard happened to him.

He found out that his wife and the pastor of the church were having an affair. The pastor was going to leave his own wife, and marry this brother's wife. Consequently his marriage ended, and his children sided with their mother. Devastated, he got into booze and drugs, yet even during this time he was a witness for his Lord and never turned his back on Jesus Christ. He even won souls to the Lord during this time he was hurting, wounded emotionally, and trying to heal. Years went by and he moved out of the area in order to get off

The Christian

the booze and drugs. He joined a good church, cleaned up, and faithfully served Jesus Christ all the days of his life.

I believe one day he will hear his Master Jesus Christ say to him, *"Well done, thou good and faithful servant. Here are some cities I want you to reign over."*

The Sons of Zadok

Chapter 6

Obededom

Great news was broadcast in the land of the Philistines - -we have defeated Israel and have captured the golden ark! It now sits in the temple of Dagon.

The news also quickly spread through the land of Israel, bringing about fear and crying. The two sons of Eli, the high priest of Israel, were dead. They died in the battle with Israels' enemies, the Philistines. But their death had been prophesied aforetime by Samuel after God appeared to him and told him what was going to happen.

Eli, who was almost blind, sat hunched forward on a bench, trembling for the ark of God. When he heard the crying, he asked what it meant; the man of Benjamin who had come from the battle told Eli that his two sons were dead. But what brought the biggest fear and grief to Eli was when the man said that the ark of God was taken. The ark was Eli's responsibly. It was the center

The Sons of Zadok

of all things spiritual for Israel, and now on his watch it was taken.

Grief, fear, and sorrow overwhelmed Eli. Eli was 98 years old and a fat man. When the news came to him, he bolted upright out of shock. This caused him to fall over backwards off the bench and broke his neck so that he died.

Then Phinehas, one of Eli's sons, wife heard about the ark as well; she was pregnant. The news caused her to go into labor. As she was giving birth she dies, but not before she names her child Ichabod, which means, "**The glory is departed.**"

> [21] And she named the child Ichabod, saying, **The glory is departed** from Israel: because the ark of God was taken, and because of her father in law and her husband. (1 Sam. 4:21)

Earlier that day the battle had ended. On the ground, wallowing in their blood lay the two wicked sons of Eli, Hophni and Phinehas. Slain by the Philistines, who were being used by God to bring forth judgement upon the wickedness of Israel. No doubt with cheers of praise for Dagon, the false god of the Philistines, they picked up the ark and carried it back to the capitol city of the Philistines: Ashdod.

There in Ashdod was the temple of Dagon: a grand, ornate temple decorated with gold, purple and green colors. At the front of the grand main hall was the statue of Dagon. You see, Dagon was the fish god that the Philistines worshipped. He was half man and half sea serpent with a fishes tail. From the waist up he was man, and from the waist down he was a fish. Similar to a mermaid, but only a man.

Obededom

The Philistines gloated as they brought the shiny golden ark into the hall of Dagon and set it by Dagon upon the altar. With a shout of, *"Hail Dagon! Praise be to Dagon, who has given us the victory today over Israel. We present you with this golden ark. The golden ark of Israel."*

It was a festive night as all of the Philistine empire celebrated their great victory over Israel. After their revelry was over and the night faded into early morning, a priest of Dagon came to open the doors to the temple. With anticipation he looked inside, and much to his horror the statue of Dagon was fallen upon his face before the ark of the Lord. He then ran and told the rest of the priests what he had seen. Then they ran into the temple and sure enough, Dagon was upon his face before the ark.

After getting help, they set Dagon back upon his throne in the temple beside the ark of the Lord. Perplexed in their minds, they wondered how that had happened. There had been no earthquake that night so it didn't make sense to them. They wondered, and a twinge of fear seemed to break into their souls, though they didn't know why.

The next morning as the doors of the temple were opened, it happened again that Dagon was fallen off his throne. But this time his arms were cut off as well as his head. Only the stump of Dagon remained.

Then strange things began to happen in Ashdod. The people were **"being destroyed"** by God.

> [6]But the hand of the LORD was heavy upon them of Ashdod, and **he destroyed them,** and **smote them with emerods,** *even* Ashdod and the coasts thereof. (1 Sam. 5)

The Sons of Zadok

It is likely that many of the people were dying. Along with that, many people were ending up with emerods. Whatever emerods are, they were in their "**secret parts.**" (1 Sam. 5:9). It is likely, though not absolute, that they were hemorrhoids. Likely a judgement of God upon the activities of the Philistines.

As things progressively got worse around Ashdod, the people began to realize that since the ark came to town all these things had begun to happen. Soon there was a cry of *"Get the ark out of here! Send it to Gath."*

The news spread quickly through the city of Gath. The morning paper had giant headlines, "Ark of Israel is Coming to Gath." What had only a few weeks earlier been cause for celebration, now was met with great concern. But it was not absolute because the judgement had only happened in one town. Perhaps the people entertained the thought, *"Maybe it was a coincidence. After all, it is a golden Ark and worth a very, very large amount of money. It is beautiful to look at. Maybe the problems in Ashdod were because those people are so wicked."*

Soon after the arrival of the ark in Gath though, things began to go downhill fast in that city. Again there was great destruction, and men were dying; the ones that weren't dying had emerods in their secret parts same as the men in Ashdod. Fear again spread through the city and they with one voice shouted, *"Get rid of that thing!! That Jewish Ark before we all die!"* So they carried the Ark out of Gath and brought it to Ekron. But by now word had spread, and the Ark was like a hot potato that nobody wanted.

As it came to Ekron, the people already knew what would happen, and they did not want it. So they

Obededom

consulted with their wise men about what to do. They told them to send the Ark away and put five golden mice and five golden emerods with the Ark as a trespass offering. And so they did.

The reason for the mice was that mice had greatly multiplied in the brief time the Ark was in the land of the Philistines. Those rodents had marred, or ruined much of the land. The Black Death, or bubonic plague, could have easily been spreading during this time, with people falling sick and dying quickly.

The Ark had remained in the land of the Philistines seven months. During this time there was a man in the city of Gath that had observed all that happened to the people. He was possibly a prominent man in the city. He noticed the judgements upon Dagon. And when he did, he realized that the God of Israel was stronger than Dagon. Then he noticed the judgements upon Ashdod, Gath, and Ekron. And as he watched, he prayed and realized that the God of Israel was the true God.

Finally the day came that the Ark was going to leave the land of the Philistines. The five golden mice had been made along with the five golden emerods. A new cart had been built, and two milk kine were tied to the cart. Normally a nursing momma cow will not leave her baby. The test would be that if the milk kine walked away from their babies with a straight course toward Israel, then they would know that all the affliction was from the Lord. If the milk kine did not do this, but wandered out of the way, then they figured it was but chance. This was the final test to see if it was an act of God or not.

It was a big day with the leaders of the land, and the lords of the Philistines assembling in their best clothes.

The Sons of Zadok

The wise men and diviners were there present as well. And among these leaders was this prominent man by the name of Obededom. Obededom was a Gittite, hence a Philistine. Gath was his home town. He was well respected, and had family there as well as many friends. But there was something different about Obededom this day. He had his wife and children with him, and it looked like they were ready for a trip with bags of clothes and things.

One of his friends looked at him with curiosity and wondered why he had brought all that luggage? Walking over to Obededom he spoke up and asked: *"Hey Obee, what are you doing with all your things and family here? You look like you a fixing' to move?"*

Obededom, trying to be a bit coy because he wasn't sure what was going to happen. Would he and his family be leaving their home that day, or would they be staying? He did not know his reply was vague, *"Well, you never know. I might me."*

Not satisfied with that answer his friend, still trying to pin him down on what he was doing pressed him some more. *"What do you mean you might be? Are you crazy? This is your home, and you're a leader here. You can't just up and leave. Besides, your children have a lot of friends here. Where would you go? Have you lost your mind? After all, you are not a Jew! You have no place in Israel. Obee, get ahold of yourself! You're not thinking straight."*

Obededom, still being coy, opened up a little more to him, *"Well, we will see. It all depends on what happens today. And you're probably right, we won't be going*

Obededom

anywhere."

As Obededom finished talking his voice did not sound so sure. In His heart he already knew that the God of the Ark was the true God. He realized that the morning he saw Dagon flat on his face. Realization overcame him that morning and then determination that he wasn't going to worship a fake god. He wanted the truth and to worship the true God.

The lords of the Philistines along with the other dignitaries stared with fearful concern at the golden box that was covered by two golden-winged cherubim. It was such a beautiful sight that it was hard not to stare at it. It was an object a person would never get to look at again in their life. And as they stared at the beauty, there was a presence and a power that radiated from it that could be felt. A power that brought a sobering fear as well as a remembrance of the stories of how God had parted the waters of the Red Sea; and how the Ark had led the way in the battle of Jericho. The longer they stared at the Ark, the more they felt like they should be on their knees, bowing to the Lord God Jehovah.

Finally, as a hush spread across the people, a man walked up to the milk kine, the mama cows. Hooked up to them was the new cart, and on the cart were the golden Ark, gold mice and gold emerods glistening in the sunshine. It truly was a beautiful, almost mesmerizing sight, as gold is always a beautiful thing to look at. Then with a loud shout and a slap on the rear of one of the cows, they started off, moooooing all the way. And as they went, they went the straight way to Bethshemesh, a city of the Jews.

The Sons of Zadok

When Obededom saw it all, he knew immediately what he was going to do. He looked at his wife and kids and said, *"Let's go."* Without hesitation, Obededom's whole family stepped out from the crowd and began to follow the Ark. They were all alone as a family, yet they did not stop. Friends from Gath began to provoke them yelling to them, *"Where are you going? What are you doing? Are you crazy?"*

To this Obededom, determined and unhesitatingly yelled back, *"We have decided to follow the true God. We no longer follow Dagon."*

Indignant replies from the crowd began to be hurled at them, *"Then go and good riddance. We don't want you around here anyway, if you're going to forsake Dagon."*

Tears came into the eyes of some of the children when they heard what was yelled at them, but they knew as well what they were to do, for Obededom had explained it all to them. And with that they followed the Ark, not knowing where they would end up, but knowing that the God of the Ark was the true God. Wherever he was, was where they wanted to be.

As the Ark came into a field of Bethshemesh, the people rejoiced to see it. When the kine stopped in the middle of the field, the men made an altar from the wood of the cart, and offered the kine upon it as a sacrifice to the Lord.

But the men of Bethshemesh didn't fear the Lord as they ought. With curiosity they decided to look into the Ark and when they did, God smote 50,000 men and they died. The people then said, *"Get that thing out of*

Obededom

here." So the Ark left, and Obededom and his family followed it further, until it ended up in Kearjath-jearem, where it was placed in the house of Abinadad. His son Eleazar, was sanctified to take care of the Ark, and it remained in the house for twenty years.

> ²And it came to pass, while the ark abode in Kirjathjearim, that the time was long; for it was twenty years: and all the house of Israel lamented after the LORD. (1Sam. 7:2)

During this time Obededom took his family, and because he wasn't a Jew, he had to build a house outside of town. Unknowingly led by God, he built his house beside the road that led straight to Jerusalem. There on a hill not far off the road he built his house and raised his family. Because they were not Jewish, the kids did not have many friends. And as the years went by his wife at times would get discouraged. Along with the discouragement she would be lonely, not having friends, so she would tearfully ask him, *"How long are we going to stay here? Why are we here? Do you even know what you are doing?"*

To this Obededom would look into her eyes with love, and with a gentle firmness reply, *"No, I don't know, but I do know that the God of the Ark is the true God and we are going to have to trust that He will guide us at His time. We have food and clothes. He has always provided, and I believe He always will."*

Along with this, every few months Obededom would gather his family together and they would go on a field trip. It was a trip to the house of Abinadab. Though they were not allowed inside, yet they would stand

The Sons of Zadok

outside, and with excitement and amazement in his voice, Obededom would tell his children about the day the Ark left Gath. He would tell them about all the miracles and judgements that God brought upon the Philistines, and then as he was finishing his stories he would get very serious and look at his family and say, *"Don't ever forget that the God of the Ark is the true God."*

Year after year they lived outside of the town. Five years, ten years, fifteen years, and it seemed there was no reason why they had done what they had. They had left family and friends. Obededom no longer made good money. They had to farm and live off the land. It was a hard life, with very few friends. After twenty years it appeared like Obededom had done a very foolish thing.

One day though, news spread; as Obededom was coming out of the fields of wheat a man went by and said, *"Hey, Obededom, did you hear the news? David is coming tomorrow to get the Ark and take it up to Jerusalem."* Obededom replied, *"Thank you for letting me know. Thank you so much!"*

Obededom burst through the front door of his house like a whirlwind and loudly said, *"Hey, everyone come here I've got news! King David is coming to get the Ark and take it to Jerusalem tomorrow. We are going to have a chance to see the Ark as it goes by. I want every one to get a bath and put on your best clothes, for tomorrow is going to be a great day."*

With that the family got busy and started getting cleaned up and ready for the event. And down in the heart of Obededom he seriously wondered, *"But what are we going to do? Why should we live here anymore if*

Obededom

the Ark is not here?" Then he said a quick prayer, *"Oh God, I am not worthy that you should hear me, but if you hear me, what should I do? If your Ark is gone from here, what and where should we go?"*

Early the next morning Obededom and his family got ready for the big day. With their best clean clothes on, they stood out in front of their house. It was right beside the main road, and they would have a front row seat to see all the action. A couple hours after sunrise King David and his men came and passed by the house to go down to the house of Abinadab. It was a grand procession with everyone in their best uniforms. David the king, in his royal robe, radiated all the beauty and majesty of any earthly monarch that ever was. Group after group marched by, and in the center of it all was a brand new cart with much gold all over it. This was the cart the Ark would be carried on, and finally the whole procession had passed. Oh my, what a glorious sight it was! And Obededom knew that they would pass by again on their way back to Jerusalem.

Other people lined the road in anticipation to see king David and the Ark of Israel. This was a once in a lifetime event, and many people had come. With great excitement people looked down the road towards Kirjathjearim to see if they could see David and his men with the Ark. Then words were shouted up the line. *"They have left the house and are on their way. Uzza and Ahio, the sons of Abinadab are driving the cart."*

It wouldn't be long now. It had been twenty years since Obededom had seen the golden Ark, and now today He was going to get to see it again; he was so excited. But in his heart he wondered what he was

191

The Sons of Zadok

going to do after the Ark left. Where would he go? He did not have the answer to these questions. Nevertheless, he was excited to see the Ark once again.

Finally the sounds of music, voices praising God, and shouting was faintly heard in the distance. Slowly it grew louder and louder. Then they saw the group as they got closer and closer. There was David the king dancing and praising God. Behind him was the Ark shining as beautiful as ever. The musicians loudly played joyful music. It was such a grand procession! It was a scene that was etched in the minds of all who were their, never to be forgotten.

With Obededom and his family right out front of their house, the event finally arrived. It was beautiful as David played, danced and passed by being just a few feet away.

People had come from miles to see the Ark and King David. They lined the road to get a glimpse of it all, but there was Someone else beside the road that day. He was there though nobody saw Him. It was the Lord, and He was not very happy with what was going on. In spite of having the scriptures, David and his men were transporting the Ark just like the heathen Philistines did, instead of going about it scripturally. The Ark was to be carried only by the priests. There were poles that slid through metal circle guides on the side of the Ark, and the poles were to be slid in and hoisted up on the shoulders of the priests. No, God was not too happy with things that day.

So as the oxen, that were pulling the cart which held the Ark, were passing by the house of Obededom, God stuck out His foot and tripped the oxen. (Yes, I know

Obededom

the Bible does not say this, but it is not coincidence that the oxen tripped in from of Obededom's house.) As the oxen stumbled, the cart tipped and Uzza, (the man driving the cart), saw what was happening and reached back to steady the Ark so it didn't fall. When he did, God smote him that he died.

Slumping over, he fell off the cart onto the road. Ahio, who was walking alongside, stopped the cart in fear, and the whole procession halted. Dancing and praising God in front of the cart, David was not aware of what had happened. Then someone yelled to him, *"Your Majesty, stop. Look!"*

Hearing that David stopped, turned around and saw Uzza on the ground dead. David's joyful face soon turned to a face of fear and trouble. Stunned silence swept through the crowd that just a few moments earlier had been filled with praise, joyful music, and happiness. All were staring at Uzza's body laying on the ground.

David's mind raced as his thoughts were troubled, *"What have I done? God, what is wrong? Why did this happen?"* A whisper of voices spread through the crowd with one word, *"Bethshemesh."* They began to fear they would all die.

David's thoughts were cloudy, *"Something about the priests carrying it on the staves. We have not moved the Ark properly."* Then David realized his error. He had not followed God's specific law on how to transport the Ark. David then cried out, *"Oh Lord, please, have mercy on us."*

The crowd seemed frozen in place. Fear had gripped all the people knowing they could be dead any moment. Then, one of David's men delicately walked over to him

The Sons of Zadok

and asked in a whisper, *"Your majesty, What are we going to do?"*

To this David replied, *"We are not bringing the Ark up to Jerusalem today."*

David's man quickly nodded his head, *"Yes, your majesty, I agree, but what are we going to do?"*

David glanced again at the dead body of Uzza where it still lay. It was a testament to the holiness of God and His wrath upon all who disobey, especially when they ought to know better. His reply was short, *"I don't know."*

Then a local man by the name of Kenan reverently approaches and says to King David, *"Your majesty, Do you see that man and his family over there in front of that house?"*

David's eyes moved off of the dead body of Uzza. Slowly finding the house and family of Obededom he replied, *"Yes, I see him. Who is he? Why do you want me to see him"*

Kenan continued, *"That man is Obededom. He left Gath to follow the Ark when the Lord brought it back to Israel. He is a good man and has lived here since the Ark came. Do you think he would take the Ark into his house. He is a Gittite, so if he gets killed at least it's not a Jew."*

David thoughtfully listened and began to nod his head at the wisdom of the words. *"Good idea. Go ask him if he would watch the Ark for us."*

Kenan was thrilled that he was able to help the King. With all eyes upon him, he walked over to Obededom and said, *"Obededom?"*

Humbly, and with great wonder Obededom answered,

Obededom

"Yes."

Kenan, now with a bit more confidence because he was serving his king, *"Would you be willing to watch the Ark for us for a while?"*

Obededom's heart just about lept out of his chest. Never in his wildest dreams had he thought he would have the Ark abide in his house. Wondering if he had heard him correctly he asked, *"You want me to watch the Ark? You mean bring it into my house?"*

Kenan, who was also acquainted with Obededom replied, *"Y..Y..Yes, yes exactly. Would you be wiling to do that?"*

Obededom, now with great joy, though still in amazement that such a thing could actually be happening to him and his family replied, *"Yes sir! I would be humbled and thrilled to do that."*

(It is interesting to note that Obededom was not afraid to take the Ark into his house, even though there was a man laying on the ground dead. Obededom has a clear conscience.) With that Kenan quickly walked over to King David and said, *"Obededom is thrilled and more than willing to watch the Ark."*

David was amazed at the calm assurance this Gittite had and wondered, *"Why was he not afraid?"* Then David spoke with a certain fear in his voice, *"OK, carry it into his house."*

With that Kenan went back over to Obededom and said, *"Obededom, we are going to carry the Ark into your house. Where do you want us to put it?"*

Obededom was overwhelmed with joy. He was not afraid, even though he had been at Bethshemesh, and this day seeing God kill Uzza. With the peace of God

The Sons of Zadok

that sleeps in a thunderstorm he knew exactly where to have the Ark set down in his house. *"I will lead you to the place. I know just the place where I will put it. Give me just one minute."*

With that, Obededom ran into the house and in his main living room he had a table. It was the table where his family knelt at for twenty years and prayed to God. It was there that he lead the men who carried it into his house.

Obededom couldn't believe his eyes. There in front of him was the Ark. He had left his home, his family, his friends, and his job to follow the Ark, and now it was with him in his living room.

David and his men humbly left and headed for Jerusalem.

Over the next three months everything Obededom did was blessed by God. During that time, David did some Scripture study and realized what he had done wrong. Upon realizing it, he prayed and begged God for forgiveness for not serving God according to scripture, as well as not fearing the Lord properly.

^{12}And it was told king David, saying, **The LORD hath blessed the house of Obededom,** and all that pertaineth unto him, because of the ark of God. So David went and brought up the ark of God from the house of Obededom into the city of David with gladness. (2 Sam. 6:12)

As the messenger from the king approached the door, he could hear singing and praising the Lord going on from inside the house. It was a joyful, clean, and pure sound that he heard, and it put a smile upon his face. His mind then was brought back to the task at hand,

Obededom

and he became more serious once again. Straightening himself up to his full height, he knocked on the door.

Inside the house Obededom wondered, *"Who could that be?"* Upon opening the door, he found a man in stately attire standing before him. This was obviously a messenger from the King.

The messenger, with an attitude of duty, then spoke and asked, *"Are you Obededom?"*

Obededom, wondering what this could be about, spoke up, *"Yes, I am."*

The messenger again out of a serious duty for the king replied, *"I have a message from King David. In three days the king is coming to take up the Ark and bring it to Jerusalem. He should arrive in the morning. Whatever you need to do, do it so you and your house will be ready for the king to pick up the Ark."*

Obededoms' countenance became solemn and in a soft reply he said, *"Yes sir, we will be ready."*

And with that the messenger turned around and left.

Slowly shutting the door, Obededom turned around, his mind and heart filled with sorrow. His wife and children had gathered and were all staring at him. His wife, seeing the look on his face spoke up and asked, *"Who was that? What did he want?"*

Obededom, almost distracted by his thoughts as his mind raced, hesitated and then said, *"It was a messenger from King David. They are coming in three days to fetch up the Ark and take it to Jerusalem."*

Obededom had left his home land and followed the Ark of the Lord. He had endured shunning and rejection of his family by those around him. Yet he had stood his ground and remained faithful, only knowing

The Sons of Zadok

that the God of the Ark was the true God. Obededom just wanted to worship and follow the true God. He desired that for his family as well.

He never imagined the Ark would one day reside in his house, but it did. His life and his family had been changed immensely by the presence of God in his home. But now the Ark was leaving. He knew it was right for the Ark to be in Jerusalem, but oh, how he longed to be close to where it was! But he wasn't a Jew. What could he do?

With a heavy heart Obededom went out into a field behind his house and fell on his knees and prayed. *"Oh Lord, what can I do? I love you and I have no regrets for following you and your Ark. I thank you Lord for coming into my house. I know I am not worthy at all. Dear Lord, would you please show me what you want me to do?"*

On and on he prayed in the field. Inside the house the family, too, was sad as they contemplated the thoughts of the Ark leaving their house. It had been the greatest time of their lives during these past three months. And now it was coming to an end. Would they go back to Gath? Would they stay there just outside of Kirjath-jearem? They did not know.

Then finally the day arrived, and the family again was in their best clothes. The great company of King David had arrived. The priests were there. The mighty men were there. And David the king was there, but this time David was very, very serious.

As the priests came into the house, Obededom and his family stood aside and let them place the poles in the side of the Ark. Then, with all seriousness, they

Obededom

raised the Ark up and slowly, reverently, and fearfully carried the Ark outside.

^{25}So David, and the elders of Israel, and the captains over thousands, went to bring up the ark of the covenant of the LORD **out of the house of Obededom with joy.** (1 Chr. 15:25)

After only six steps, David called for sacrifices to be made. With that also David danced before the Lord with all of his might. Then just as they were getting ready to proceed farther up the road to Jerusalem, Obededom looked over at the king as if he had been trying to get his attention. Finally the king saw him and came over to speak with Obededom.

King David, now had a great respect for Obededom. *"Obededom, I've heard about all that you have done by leaving Gath, your home land and following the Ark all these years. I was impressed and relieved that you were willing to keep the Ark for these past three months."*

Obededom humbly bowed on his knees to the King. It was a long shot but he had to try. He had brought his family all this way, so he had to give it a try. By faith he spoke up: *"Your majesty, you know what the Lord did unto Dagon in Ashdod, and how He brought judgements upon the people wherever the Ark went. When I saw that I knew that the Lord God Jehovah was the true God and I have followed Him ever since.*

I never dreamed He would allow me to keep the Ark, but he has."

King David could see that Obededom's eyes had filled with tears and wondered why. Then Obededom spake again, *"Your majesty, I know that I am not a Jew. I am*

The Sons of Zadok

merely a gentile dog. I know that. But could I and my family come with you to Jerusalem? We have lived by the ark for over twenty years and the thought of being away from the ark, and especially God's presence, breaks our hearts."

King David settled his countenance and sent up a quick prayer:

"Lord, would you want this man to come to Jerusalem? I can see how you have blessed him and there is no doubt that he and his family love you. They have left every thing, endured rejection, loneliness, and poverty just to be close to the ark. It is obvious you have blessed him and his family."

Before David was through praying, the Lord spoke to his heart and said, "Let him come with the ark to Jerusalem."

David was a little surprised, so He asks the Lord, "Let him come?"

The Lord, a little more firmly replied, "That is what I said, yes, let him come."

David obediently responds, "Yes sir Lord. I will do that."

David then looked at Obededom and said, "Obededom, the Lord said it was OK for you to come with the ark to Jerusalem, along with your family."

Joy sprung up in the face of Obededom. He shouted "Halleluiah," and then turned to his family, who were a little ways off, and loudly said, "The Lord has said we can come to Jerusalem!"

The kids hugged each other, and he ran and hugged their momma. Tears of joy ran down their cheeks. They could proceed to live where the ark would be.

Obededom

> ³⁷So he left there before the ark of the covenant of the LORD Asaph and his brethren, to minister before the ark continually, as every day's work required:
>
> ³⁸And **Obededom with their brethren,** threescore and eight; Obededom also the son of Jeduthun and Hosah *to be* porters... (1 Chr. 16:37-38)

You will notice that there are two Obededoms. But with the first one there is no genealogy given, and he is said to be **"with their brethren."**

> ⁴Moreover the sons of Obededom *were,* Shemaiah the firstborn, Jehozabad the second, Joah the third, and Sacar the fourth, and Nethaneel the fifth,
>
> ⁵Ammiel the sixth, Issachar the seventh, Peulthai the eighth: **for God blessed him.** (1 Chr. 26:4-5)

They were porters, as in transporters and those who carried the furniture around. These would be strong men for this type of work. And then there is a very curious verse in the word of God.

> ²⁴And *he took* all the gold and the silver, and all the vessels that were found in the house of God **with Obededom,** and the treasures of the king's house, the hostages also, and returned to Samaria. (2 Chr. 25:24)

Isn't that strange? Why? Well, because when these vessels were carried away it was hundreds of years later. Yet, they are said to be with Obededom. It looks like Obededom was buried with the vessels and furniture of the house of God. He worked and gave his

201

The Sons of Zadok

life in service for the house of his God.

I have always pictured Obededom when he had arrived in Jerusalem. Maybe he had been there for a year or so. One day King David came out to the tabernacle to worship the Lord. As he approached the outside of the area Obededom opened a gate for the king to let him come into the area. As he did David stopped and looked at Obededom asking:

"Obee? Do you ever get tired of merely opening this gate and working around here?"

With that Obededom smiled. *"No sir, your majesty! I had rather be a doorkeeper in the house of my God, than to dwell in the tents of wickedness."*

David looked at him and thoughtfully, nodding in agreement. *"You're a good man Obededom. Carry on."*

And as David walked on by he thought about what Obededom had just said. He then said to himself, *"I need to write that down."*

[10] For a day in thy courts is better than a thousand. **I had rather be a doorkeeper in the house of my God, than to dwell in the tents of wickedness.** (Psa. 84:10)

The years rolled on, and Obededom died. He rested in Paradise with the rest of the saints. He followed the Lord to Heaven when Jesus led captivity captive that first day of the week when He arose and ascended to Heaven.

So now let's move forward 2500 years. The Lord Jesus Christ has returned to the earth and is setting up His kingdom. Before Him the earth is being cleaned up, regenerated, and made again as the garden of Eden. Along with that jobs are being given out, and rewards

Obededom

for the faithful are being awarded.

Sitting upon the throne of His glory is the King of Kings, the Lord Jesus Christ. And here comes Obededom. He kneels before the King. The King then speaks and calls his name, *"Obededom."*

Obededom replies, *"Yes, Your Majesty."*

King Jesus, with fondness and kindness towards the one kneeling in front of Him speaks, *"Obededom, well done, thou good and faithful servant. You were faithful to Me in your heart as well as in your service. You left your family, friends and all that you had to follow Me. There was no doubt that I was, and am the true God, yet you and a few others were the only ones who left Dagon, and Gath to follow Me. You loved the house of God and the Ark. You loved My presence and were not afraid to take in the Ark which had the presence of God on it. So now I have a special place for you in My Kingdom. Instead of serving and being told what to do, you are going to tell every one else what to do and how to do it. You will reign with Me.*

I know you always wanted to take care of the Ark and the things of the temple. I knew I could always trust you to do the right thing. So now you will reign with me in the center of the world for 1000 years."

The Sons of Zadok

LIST OF WORKS BY THE AUTHOR

All works are available through online stores and physical stores.

1. **HERE COMES THE BRIDE**, A Critique of the Baptist Bride Heresy. 174 pages

2. **Good Vibrations**, Overcoming Spasmodic Dysphonia, 218 Pages

3. **DEFILED**, The Spiritual Dangers of Alternative Medicine, 351 pages

4. **AROMATHERAPY**, From a Biblical Perspective, 236 pages

Sermon in a Book Series

1. **JESUS, TALK TO ME**, Have you ever desired to get the Lord's attention?, 54 Pages

2. **DEALING WITH BAD IN-LAWS**, A Bible study on Jacob and Laban, 116 Pages

3. **EVEN AS GOD**, Healing relationships Biblically, 190 Pages

4. **FOUR SIDES OF CALVARY**, Our Lord's Battle on the Cross, 84 Pages

5. **The Sons of Zadok,** What Will You Do for 1000 Years?

www.ingramcontent.com/pod-product-compliance
Lightning Source LLC
Chambersburg PA
CBHW050316120526
44592CB00014B/1934